Barks and V 🐾 W9-BGN-697

Listen Like a Dog . . .

"*Listen Like a Dog* offers a totally fresh perspective on attaining success in our personal and professional relationships. Jeff Lazarus gives you the tools to get out of your own way and experience the miracles that will come to you when you model the behavior of man's best friend. The witty and wise advice he offers will enable you to become a master communicator in almost any situation. Take the lead from your dog and reap the rewards."

—**Jack Canfield**, co-creator of the *Chicken Soup for the Soul* series and creator of *The Success Principles* series

"There's a reason so many people have a strong bond with their dog. A dog's full attention invites us to share more of our real selves with them, and opens the way for pure and positive communication—even if it is nonverbal. Jeff Lazarus has given us a roadmap to living a happier and more productive life with this invaluable book. His tongue-in-cheek style will leave you laughing, but ultimately make you realize that your canine companion seriously has much to teach you about how to become a better listener!"

—**Dr. Marty Becker**, "America's veterinarian" and *New York Times* bestselling author

"There is no doubt that the ability to listen—to really, authentically listen—is one of the most important qualities of an effective leader, top salesperson, good friend, and successful family member. Who in the world, however, would believe that the very best teacher of this vital skill would be . . . our dog? Well, actually, practically anyone and everyone who has ever had a dog! In this terrific book, told through the eyes of a true dog-lover and expert on the topic of listening, we learn how to master the skill applied so naturally by our canine children."

—**Bob Burg**, coauthor of *The Go-Giver*

"Chew on this: your dog is your mindfulness guru! You will bow, and say WOW, when you learn how."

—**Michael J. Gelb**, author of
How to Think Like Leonardo da Vinci

Listen Like a Dog

Listen Like a Dog

. . . and Make Your Mark
on the World

JEFF LAZARUS

Health Communications, Inc.
Deerfield Beach, Florida

www.hcibooks.com

Library of Congress Cataloging-in-Publication Data
is available through the Library of Congress

© 2016 Jeff Lazarus

ISBN-13: 978-07573-1898-6 (Paperback)
ISBN-10: 07573-1898-3 (Paperback)
ISBN-13: 978-07573-1899-3 (ePub)
ISBN-10: 07573-1899-1 (ePub)

Publisher: Health Communications, Inc.
        3201 S.W. 15th Street
        Deerfield Beach, FL 33442–8190

Cover design by Jeff Lazarus
Illustrations by Steve Feldman
Interior formatting by Lawna Patterson Oldfield

Thank you to all of the dogs who have
listened to me bark over the years;
I always ended up feeling better.

Contents

Acknowledgments

All of my knowledge and abilities in the art of listening can
be attributed to my dearly departed listening guru, a gold-colored,
four-legged fur angel named Roamy; the funniest, smartest, and
cutest being I have ever known. Roamy's contributions to my life
are with me every day and I miss him dearly.

The endless love and support from D.E. helped to make this possible; you're the best! Thank you, A.W., for your friendship, your
support, and for pointing out the obvious to me; this is a book that
I've been writing my whole life. Thank you to the folks at HCI for
loving dogs and helping me to spread the word about the importance
of listening. Those who have believed in me and encouraged me over
the years, in any of my endeavors, should know that they have had
a positive impact on me and my work. I have been blessed to have
had the experience of being truly listened to over the years, mainly
by dogs, and a few humans along the way; and it's always been a

rewarding experience. It's now my desire to make the world a better place, one listener at a time.

Thank you to dogs everywhere. Without you there would be a lot less joy, happiness, and fun in the world. . . . and squeak toys and liver treats.

Roamy, my "listening guru." Here he is on his first Thanksgiving, fresh from the backyard and guilty as can be—with evidence of his infraction still on his nose. He may have denied knowing who was digging in the garden, but he sure listened to me when I asked him about it.

INTRODUCTION

Learn from the Master— Man's Best Listener

*There is no psychiatrist in the world
like a puppy licking your face.*

—Ben Williams

Have you ever *talked* to a dog? Not just the "Who's a good boy? Spike's a good boy" stuff, but really talked? About your struggles, your heartaches, your joys? Have you ever thrown self-consciousness to the wind and bared your soul to a canine friend?

If not, you might want to try it. No appointment necessary, no co-pay required. Well, maybe a walk or a treat . . .

If you have talked to a dog this way, how did it make you feel?

You probably felt *free*. Free to say whatever you wanted to say, without the burden of making logical sense, justifying your position, or having to tell an entertaining story. Free to feel whatever you needed to feel.

You probably felt *unrushed*. As if you had all the time in the world to speak your piece—and your listener wasn't checking his watch or cell phone and edging toward the door.

No doubt you felt *accepted* and *un-judged*. You could have confessed to a triple homicide and your listener wouldn't have held it against you.

Odds are you felt *supported*, as if your listener was on *your* side. You felt positive, compassionate energy coming your way.

You probably felt as if you were the center of another being's world, the most important thing in that being's life, at least at that moment. You almost certainly felt a *connection* with that being: a life-to-life connection uncomplicated by abstract concepts, such as credit card bills or dinner plans or the fight you had last night.

Most of all, you felt *heard*. Received. Taken in. Though your listener may not have understood the words you were literally saying, he heard *you*—the person *behind* the words and feelings. And so you felt complete in your communication.

When was the last time you felt that way talking to a fellow human being?

When was the last time someone felt that way after talking to *you*?

Couldn't the world use a little more of this kind of listening? A *lot* more?

Real Connection: Where Did It Go?

We live in the Era of Connectivity—or so we're told. Over the past few decades, trillions of technology dollars have been invested in developing cool new ways for humans to connect with one another. With each new connectivity platform that emerges—cell phones, chat rooms, e-mail, voicemail, instant messaging, texting, Skype, Facebook, Twitter, online gaming, etc.—the community of mankind grows closer to us. Our cell phone and e-mail contacts often number in the hundreds, and many of us have hundreds, or even *thousands,* of LinkedIn connections, Facebook friends, and/or Twitter followers. We hold the world, almost literally, in the palm of our hands. How unbelievably awesome!

Well . . . maybe . . .

So how are we using all this new technology? Do we suddenly have more meaningful things to say to one another? Are we breaking new ground in our personal and business relationships? Have we deepened our connection to humanity at large? Do we have more intimate friends?

Um . . . well . . .

A recent study reported by *ABC News* revealed that we actually have fewer real friends than we did before the social networking boom:[1] a full one-third fewer, to be precise, since 1985. Friendship, for the purposes of the study, was defined simply as someone you could talk to about "important matters." Think about that. Our ability to *confide* in one another—to be honest, direct, open, and real—is shrinking. With all the connectivity at our fingertips, we don't have *more* true communion with our fellow beings, we have *less.*

What's going on here? There has been an unprecedented explosion in our *number* of connection points, yet a drastic reduction of real connections. We have superficial, trivialized connections with more and more people, but deep, real connections with fewer and fewer.

---

1 *http://abcnews.go.com/Technology/facebook-friends-fewer-close-friends-cornell-sociologist/story?id =14896994#.UcwOF-DTk1E*

Face it: when you realize that the three orcs in your raiding party in *World of Warcraft* are your most intimate friends, it's time to admit that something has gone off the rails.

This quantity-over-quality sellout does not affect only our personal lives, it affects our business lives as well. It has long been known that personal connections are the key ingredient that sells products, brings teams together, and tips the decision-making scales one way or another. Those old-timey *Death of a Salesman* guys who spent half their lives on the road, visiting customers and taking them out for dinner and drinks, might have known a thing or two. That is, people do business with people they like and feel connected to. The same is true with hiring decisions. It's well known that employers often hire the people they like. We want to work with people with whom we feel a connection. That basic fact hasn't changed in the digital era.

And yet we all seem to be drinking the Kool-Aid of superficiality. We point proudly at our bloated "friends" lists, but many of us have no one to call when we need a *real* friend. Instead, we post our woes on Facebook, looking for comfort.

The Missing Ingredient

Humans are a social species. That's just the way we're wired. Connections with other living beings are what feed us, sustain us, validate us, and bring us joy, comfort, and meaning. Multiple studies demonstrate that those who are cut off from others, either physically or emotionally, suffer more depression and other psychological disorders, get sick more often and for longer periods, and die younger than those who have thriving, meaningful connections.[2] Conversely, people with vibrant human connections are mentally and physically healthier and live longer. And the quality of their lives is reportedly much higher.

The Simple Secret to Connection

The ability to connect with other people in our personal and professional lives comes down to one essential skill. Oddly enough, it's the one skill I see lacking in a large percentage of business interactions I've witnessed, as well as most personal interactions. It's this: the willingness and ability to *listen*. Salespeople talk up their products, but don't listen to what their customers really need. Politicians boast about their records, but don't ask what their constituents are looking for in a leader. Parents blame teachers for a child's bad grades, but don't ask what their son or daughter could do differently. Facebook devotees often blare their opinions on their page, but don't ask if you care or might be offended. There's a serious lack of ability to switch gears from output mode to input mode.

Most of us modern humans have our stick shift jammed in "output." We may know how to *physically* shut our mouths (every now and then), but we haven't developed the internal spaciousness to listen. Our inner cup runneth over with our own content. And *we're* the ones who are suffering.

---

2 *http://www.health.harvard.edu/newsletter_article/the-health-benefits-of-strong-relationships*

So we have a problem here. We don't listen. But the *bigger* problem is that we don't know that we have a problem. Instead we continue to solve for the reverse, by finding even more and newer ways for our voices to (hopefully) be heard.

A Lopsided World

The vast majority of our communication training focuses on the *output* side of the equation. And yet input makes up fully half of all communications. After all, in order for successful communication to occur, a message must be sent and it must also be received. But virtually all of our focus is on the sending side. No wonder we're such crappy listeners!

I admit, the concept of listening isn't a sexy one. After all, who wants to listen to someone else when we're so in love with our own voice? Maybe it's just me, but the thought of making a connection with someone, a true connection, can be quite a sexy thing.

My undergrad degree is in speech communication. This curriculum, with an emphasis in interpersonal and organizational communication, trained me not only in various aspects of presentation skills (i.e., persuasive speaking, oral interpretation, debate) but also in areas such as interpersonal communication, critical thinking, and organizational theory. When I graduated, I felt prepared to enter the working world, armed with the knowledge and skills to have a voice in the rat race. What I wasn't taught was that poor listening was an epidemic and a limiting factor for success.

When we prepare to make a business presentation, what do we concentrate on? Content and delivery. When we attend a business meeting, we try to be the one who adds the most intelligent/creative/ insightful comments. When we go on a date, we angle to present *our* incredible life story (*yawn*). Output, output, output.

Today, thanks to technology, we swim in a virtual ocean of output. We have 700 channels of cable TV, an endless parade of blogs, and a constant tide of messages rolling through our in-boxes. On our smart devices we can click until eternity from one online commentary thread to another. We are drowning in the output of others, all of which are competing for our listening ear.

The Need to Be Heard

A nd yet . . . ask anyone what's wrong with any relationship in their life—business or personal—and the number-one answer you'll hear is that people don't feel listened to! Parents don't think their kids listen to them. Kids don't think their parents listen to them. Spouses don't feel listened to by their partners. Employees don't feel listened to by their bosses. Customers don't feel companies listen to them.

This all boils down to three simple precepts, in my view:

We're all talking, but no one is listening, and . . .

People, everywhere, want to be heard, so . . .

People are *highly attracted* to those who listen to them.

And these precepts lead to an obvious conclusion: if we want to make an impact in today's noisy world, then by far the greatest gift

Listening is the most powerful way to forge bonds with others.

we can give anyone is to *listen* to them. Listening is the single most powerful way we can forge deep and meaningful bonds with our fellow human beings, and yet it's the skill most of us seem singularly uninterested in developing.

Let's Learn from the Best

I've been a presenter on listening skills and a facilitator of listening and customer engagement workshops, which I enjoy and always learn from. Moreover, I've spent years "in the trenches," having had thousands of interactions with customers, salespeople, and thought leaders in medicine. Beyond my career, I have been fortunate to have numerous friendships and romantic relationships. In doing so, I've experienced enormous frustration from the lack of listening by others—and, admittedly, I've made lots of listening mistakes of my own—so my desire to write this book has been gaining momentum for some time.

The truth is, I am a major dog lover. I adore dogs. I have had close relationships with several four-legged friends and have also talked to hundreds of them over the years. What I've discovered, through all these canine encounters, is that dogs are among the best listeners around.

Just look at the very definition of the word *listen*. Here are three of the meanings offered on Dictionary.com:

1. **to give attention** with the ear; attend closely for the purpose of hearing; give ear.
2. **to pay attention;** heed; obey.
3. **to wait attentively** for a *sound.*

What creature comes to mind when you read those words? I don't know about you, but for me it's *Canis familiaris* all the way.

One eventful day I was talking with a friend and fellow dog lover. I was telling her about Roamy, a gold-colored, mixed-breed fur angel who graced my life for eleven precious years. Seeing Roamy at the end of my day was something I genuinely looked forward to.

Now I had always *chatted* with Roamy, but one night, for some reason, I really opened up to him about some authentic stuff—about what was going on in my life. I don't know why. I went on and on, telling Roamy about this problem and that problem, sharing my observations about the world and my fellow man. We were on the couch with the volume down on the TV. Roamy just lay there, listening in silence and beaming his nonjudgmental love and attention at me. When I finished, I felt incredibly light and *unburdened.* I really felt heard!

These little talks started to become a regular thing. Roamy became my confidant, my coconspirator, my canine healer. Once or twice a week, I'd take him into my confidence and just *talk*, knowing he didn't understand most of my words, but feeling he understood *me.*

As I was telling this story to my dog-loving friend, I began to realize what it was that had made me feel so good talking to Roamy. Much of it was in what he *didn't* do.

He didn't judge me or take sides or say, "Well, you were no picnic to live with, either." He didn't interrupt me. He didn't offer advice or try to fix my problems or say, "You'll grow from this." He didn't argue with me or correct my facts. He didn't say, "That reminds me of a time the same thing happened to me." He didn't lose focus, zone out, or look at his watch or phone (he might have nodded off once or twice, but we'll let that slide). He didn't withdraw from me or put up walls when I said something "negative." He didn't tell me to get over my damn self and move on. He didn't make mindless noises just to contribute to the conversation (I'll assume his occasional flatulence was an involuntary thing). He didn't offer platitudes such as, "This, too, shall pass," "At least you still have your health," or "Someday you'll look back on this and laugh."

Had I been talking to a human, some or all of the above would probably have happened. As a result, I would have edited myself more. I would have ended up feeling frustrated and unfulfilled. I wouldn't have been as honest or self-revealing. Seriously.

The point is, I felt more "listened to" by Roamy than I had by most humans in my life. (And this isn't just the wild imaginings of an unapologetic dog lover; scientists have recently learned that dogs' brains process the human voice in much the same way as human brains do.[3]) I realized it was the way I felt when I talked to Roamy—accepted, supported, validated—that was critical.

The message became clear to me: we humans need to learn to listen like a dog.

---

3 *http://news.sciencemag.org/brain-behavior/2014/02/how-dogs-know-what-youre-feeling*

The funny thing is, we are the ones who "bark" incessantly and get annoyed when dogs make the slightest sound. We often try to make dogs more human by putting clothes on them and making them do human things (admit it, you have), but maybe we have more to learn from them than they from us.

"But wait," you might be tempted to say. "Surely, you're not saying we should *really* listen like dogs in order to improve our listening skills?"

Well, yes, I *am* saying that. I'm not saying you need to tilt your head to the side or adjust your ears like individual antennae the way dogs do, but I am saying you should strive to be doglike in your listening approach.

Good luck with that, by the way. You see, most of us could *never come close* to listening as well as a dog. We humans are not capable of that kind of focus, presence, ego-lessness, and spaciousness. But if we could be 50 *or even 25 percent* as effective as a dog, we would be listening superstars.

Listening Like a Dog

Think about the essential qualities that make "dog listening" so special. Dogs . . .

- listen with their entire being, not just their ears
- use alert body language and make good eye contact
- send us pure, positive, loving energy
- are completely comfortable with silence

- have no agenda (unless it's time for their walk or their dish is empty)
- make us the center of their world—as if our presence were a treat for them, just like bacon!
- listen to our intentions and feelings, not just our words
- study and respond to our energy levels
- don't judge
- don't interrupt
- don't argue, lecture, or correct
- are infinitely patient
- forgive and forget
- don't get distracted by a dialogue going on in their heads—at least as far as we know (though we do occasionally lose their attention to a doorbell or a passing fire truck)
- are spontaneous and go with the flow
- are the *real deal* in an increasingly virtual world

Maybe that's why an estimated 1 million dogs in the United States alone are named as the main beneficiaries in their owners' wills.[4]

Imagine if you could do for other humans what dogs do for us. Imagine if you could be that stunningly *real* presence in a world of e-mails and text messages and rehearsed voicemails. Might this not make you your customers' favorite salesperson, your boss's go-to person, and/or a highly sought-after friend and lover?

---

4 *http://dogsears.wordpress.com/2008/05/07/100-fascinating-facts-about-dogs/*

You *can* be that kind of presence in the life of others. And you can do it, not by making more noise than anyone else; not by coming up with cleverer or sexier opening lines. You can do it by truly listening. Like a dog.

Imagine if you could do for other humans what dogs do for us.

When most of us think about making a mark in the world, we think about *producing* something worthy of attention. But in today's noisy, content-saturated world, the real way to make a mark is to penetrate the heart and mind of a fellow human being. You do that by taking the time to learn about who *they* are, what *they're* thinking, and how *they're* doing. You do it by listening like a dog.

When you truly listen to a fellow human being, you form a connection that can last forever. And once this connection has been formed, you'll have an audience for all your wonderful output when the time comes around for that.

One great thing about dogs is that they're always eager to learn new tricks. We humans, on the other hand, like to believe we're experts at everything, especially at everyday skills like listening. If you're human (and I'm guessing you are), you probably have a *lot* to learn about listening.

The challenge is: can you teach an old human a new trick?

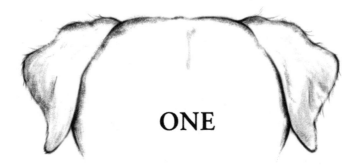

ONE

Violating the Leash Laws

LEASH LAWS

NO INTERRUPTING

NO TEXTING WHILE LISTENING

NO ONE-UPPING THE SPEAKER

NO TALKING ENDLESSLY

The more I learn about people,
the more I like my dog.

— MARK TWAIN

Let's take an honest look at the way we humans *typically* listen. Because if we don't look with open eyes at our bad habits—which I call "leash-law violations"—we'll have no motivation to learn to listen like a dog.

Again, the problem with human listeners is that (1) we all think we're already good at listening, and (2) we don't think there's anything special about listening that we need to learn.

Why is this? Well, listening was one of the first things we all learned to do as infants. Right? We were listening before we were walking, talking, or even holding our own toys. Listening seems as natural to us as breathing, so we don't even *think* of it as a skill. We think we're already experts on the topic.

But are we?

Most of us, because we've never explored what listening really is, carry around half-formed, unconscious, and primitive beliefs about the topic. Oh sure, if we're asked to define *listening*, we come up with a nice-sounding definition. But in practice we act as if listening means little more than waiting for the other person to shut up so that we can start talking.

Most of us fail to grasp the number-one purpose and goal of listening: *to understand*. This is often overlooked or not realized, but remember: the goal of listening is *to understand*.

That is what makes the art of listening so elegantly simple and yet so incredibly challenging.

It is through the simple act of *understanding* that human connections are forged. Think about it. I may work at a desk beside you for twenty years, but if we don't understand each other, you will feel no connection with me. On the other hand, I may meet you on a subway and have a quick conversation between stops. If this fleeting contact results in a moment of shared understanding, we will form a timeless connection. Understanding is king.

To listen is to seek understanding—period. It is all about the other person, not you. If you reminded yourself of this goal every time someone began to speak to you, in a matter of months you would become a Listening Master. But because we fail to grasp the true purpose of listening, or forget it in the heat of discussion, we commit several major leash-law violations.

Leash-Law Violations

What do I mean by leash-law violations? Well, in many ways, good listening is the art of putting oneself on a leash. Think for a minute about what a leash is: a simple device that accomplishes two major purposes—connection and restraint.

First, the leash *connects* two living creatures together, usually a human and a dog. When a leash is clipped to a collar, the two beings essentially become as one. They then embark on an adventure together, down the street, through the woods, through the park, or through the neighbors' yards. During the time they are thus connected, they each become the most important being in the world to the other.

The leash is also about *restraint*. The leash is used to control bad impulses, random wanderings, runaways, and hostile takeovers. Without a leash, bad habits rule the day and self-control goes out the window.

To listen well is to consciously use a "leash" on yourself: both to deliberately seek connection with another being and to restrain yourself from undisciplined behaviors.

Unfortunately, most of us leave the leash in the drawer when we enter a conversation. If only we would remember to use a leash every time we're called upon to listen, we wouldn't be guilty of so many violations—and we are all guilty of at least some of them—and we would be well on our way to listening like a dog.

If only we would remember to use a leash every time we're called upon to listen.

Typical Leash-Law Violations

1. "I'll stop you right there." (interrupting)

The number-one leash-law violation is cutting people off before they have finished speaking. We interrupt for all kinds of reasons: because we think we get it already, because we want to show the speaker we're on their wavelength, because we hear something we disagree with, or because we simply *must* throw in a devastatingly clever remark. ("'Airline *schedule*'—isn't that an oxymoron? *Ha ha ha.*") But mainly we interrupt because we've grown weary of being "walked" in the conversation and feel the need to grab the leash for a while. Our need to be heard outweighs our need to listen. We have an uncontrollable urge to bark.

When we interrupt someone, what we're really saying is that we understand their thoughts better than they do or that what they are saying isn't as important or intelligent as what we have to say. And so that person feels negated, devalued, invalidated. They shut down.

How often does a dog interrupt you when you're speaking?

2. "That's my cue!" (mentally rehearsing what to say)

Often when someone else "has the stage" (i.e., is talking), we're pacing around in the wings, rehearsing *our* big scene. We're mentally preparing what *we're* going to say next.

The moment you start preparing your own response, you stop trying to understand the other person. You're no longer listening to his/her content, but are waiting for *your cue*—the magic moment when *you* can step on stage and steal the scene. We humans may think we're good at multitasking, but it's impossible to listen and mentally rehearse at the same time. These are mutually incompatible tasks—like trying to inhale and exhale simultaneously.

Notice a dog, however, who has no interest in scene-stealing. (They don't need to, they're show-stealers naturally.)

3. "Uh-huh . . . Yeah . . . Got ya . . . Mm-hmm . . . For sure . . ." (verbal noisemaking)

Many of us think we must emit a continual stream of verbal *excreta* in order to demonstrate that we're listening. This ranges from a simple "uh-huh" and "yeah, yeah," to medium-sized non-statements like, "Yeah, I know what you mean," and "That is so true," all the way to full-scale verbal dumps.

Here we may need a muzzle along with a leash. Though it *can* be very helpful, especially on the phone, to occasionally make a noise to let your listener know you haven't wandered off to make a grilled-cheese sandwich, mindless noisemaking tells the speaker you're not really listening but rather *putting on a show* of listening.

Notice, by contrast, the exquisite silence of a dog.

4. "Why, that's fascinating . . ." (daydreaming)

Many of us, while pretending to listen, mentally wander off to someplace more interesting. Daydreaming is a great way to avoid engaging with topics or people we find . . . well, boring. After all, why listen to a client ramble on about their kid's recital last night when you can slip away to Aspen with your fantasy lover in your mind?

But, of course, people *know* when you've gone to Aspen. They may not know it consciously, but they can sense a loss of attention. That is what's so extraordinary about the way dogs listen to us. Dogs give us their full listening presence, even though they don't always understand the words we're saying.

5. "I have a cousin who likes pistachios." (derailing the conversation)

We've all met people who have an uncanny habit of derailing conversations with random side comments. We've done it ourselves. The person who is speaking makes a passing reference to a topic, and we latch on to it and launch our own line of chatter, failing to ask ourselves whether we're serving the point of the conversation. A client, for example, mentions a business operation in Scotland and you chime in, "My wife and I went to Scotland last summer. We saw wild ponies!" Suddenly the conversation is about ponies.

A dog, conversely, is happy to follow your lead.

6. "The bear that attacked me was even bigger!" (needing to "top" the other person)

One of the most obnoxious leash-law violations is the reflexive urge to outdo the person speaking. For some reason we often feel duty-bound to prove that we are smarter, funnier, more experienced, or more accomplished than the person speaking—or that we've suffered more; that's always a goodie.

If the person tells you that her child made the honor roll at school , for example, we have to come up with one that's even better. We have to launch into how our kindergartner tested into the gifted program and is already applying to Harvard. If the person mentions an illness, an injury, or a bad day they've had, we have to come up with something that tops it. "That reminds me of the time I ran out of gas on the train tracks in the desert while my wife was in labor . . ."

Dogs, on the other hand, are portraits of humility. When you're speaking, they look upon you as if you are the greatest orator in history, and they have no desire to outdo you. (Or, as author Christopher Morley put it, "No one appreciates the very special genius of your conversation as the dog does.")

7. "Be with you in juuuust a sec!" (dividing our attention)

How many times have you been speaking to someone when you catch them reading an e-mail or sending a text message under the table? "OMG, Scott really said that?" How do you feel when that happens? Have you ever seen a man watching a game on TV and telling his wife, "Go ahead, I'm listening"? Nah, that's never happened. Nowadays, in this era of multitasking, we all have constant electronic demands on our attention, but listening means giving actual mind space to that biological creature sharing the room with you. Like a dog does.

Dogs give us undivided attention—just look at their ears, eyes, and body language.

8. "I'll tell you exactly what you need to do." (offering immediate solutions)

One of our most annoying leash-law violations is to jump in and solve a person's problems before they've even finished explaining them. Guys tend to do this a lot, and it drives women insane; they listen with the goal of *fixing*, not understanding. "Just tell your sister she needs therapy." Remember: the goal of listening is to understand, not to diagnose, prescribe, fix, or solve. *After* the person has fully explained whatever problem he or she may be having, *and if* the person actively requests our help, only *then* ought we begin to offer solutions. But at the outset, the only goal is to understand.

One of the reasons we love talking to dogs is that they never try to give advice. (Except for that a walk, right now, is the solution to any problem.)

9. "The runaway train." (failing to shut our trap for three consecutive seconds)

Many of us fail to realize we have weak listening skills, because we never dust them off and give them a try. We're too busy talking. It never ceases to amaze me the way some people (most of us on occasion) simply assume that the entire point of a conversation is to talk. And they think that every time they open their mouth, they automatically have a captive audience. So they talk, and talk, and talk, and talk, and . . . well, you know how this goes.

First of all, no one owes us their attention. It is a privilege we *earn* by being gracious, thoughtful, and, yes, interesting.

Second, this is a *conversation*, not a Shakespearean soliloquy. That other person you're standing with has a mind, a tongue, and an agenda too. Perhaps they would like to take them out for a spin.

Dogs usually bark only when they have something important to announce—such as, "OH NO! THERE'S A GUY WALKING AROUND IN THE YARD NEXT DOOR!" The rest of the time they are content to hear what we have to say. And when they violate this leash law, we go crazy, elevating the infraction to a violation of one of the Ten Commandments!

10. "But you said I could . . . " (The joys of selective listening)

Have you ever wondered how someone came up with a particular conclusion based on something you said? Hundreds of times, I bet. It's a peculiar thing how one person projects a set of words into the atmosphere and the other person happens to take away a message that has you wondering what universe this is. The result of such an infraction has been the subject of conflict between parties since time began. Unfortunately these result in minor, and not-so-minor, disagreements. Imagine the happy husband who has to call off watching the game with the guys as he begrudgingly takes Briana to her classmate's birthday party, because he thought he heard . . ."

So often, we hear what we want to hear. The inner voice often plays a tune we want to hear instead of the one that is being played on the outside. After all, if we are selective about

which words we want to accept, the more we can mold the
story into something to our advantage.

11. "But you said you were fine" (listening only to the words, not the emotions)

Another egregious leash-law violation is to take the speaker's
words literally, while ignoring tone of voice, facial expression,
energy level, body language, and emotional state. A classic
example is when someone shouts back at you, "I'm fine!" in
a terse or angry tone. If we take their words literally, they get
even more upset. Why? They want us to react to the emotion,
as displayed by tone and nonverbal cues.

Dogs, lacking the crutch of verbal language, are masters at
reading emotional cues. They pay attention to the mood and
energy *behind* the words more than to the words themselves.
Try saying "good dog" to your pup in a disapproving voice.
He'll look at you as if his head is about to explode. The words
and the tone don't add up.

And that's just a small sampling of typical human "listening" tendencies. There are many more, such as finishing someone's sentence
for them, passing judgment, needing to be right more than to hear
what the person is saying, and allowing our emotional buttons to
be pushed. Most of us probably do at least three or four of them on
a chronic basis. As a result, most of us are flawed listeners. And that
is why we live in such a disconnected world.

All of the above "violations" have one thing in common: they are about making *you* the most important person in the conversation instead of the person speaking. When you do this, you invalidate, dishonor, insult, or censor the other person. You cause him/her to shut down, withdraw, or retreat. You may even create resentment.

When was the last time you saw a dog have that effect on someone? (If dogs were committing these violations, there would be far more return trips to the pound.)

Business and personal relationships, not to mention your own health and vibrancy, thrive on *connection*, which occurs when human beings understand one another. Understanding happens when you allow yourself to truly take in and experience another human being. That means listening. Listening can and will change every aspect of your life for the better.

Again, the goal of listening is to understand. Listening is a tremendous challenge, though. That's because we have all had decades of training on how *not* to do it well. (We watch our fellow man instead of our dogs!) Most of us have been trained in how to *respond*, not how to listen. So we go through life giving responses we think we're "supposed to" give, responses that seem canned and rehearsed. Dogs, on the other hand, spend their entire lives *actually* listening (i.e., paying close attention), but, oddly enough, we train them and reward them for their responses. Who has more to learn from whom?

Listening can and will change every aspect of your life for the better.

Changing your habits will require awareness and commitment, not just a one-off blast of insight. If you are lucky enough to live with a dog, however, the dog can be your constant source of inspiration and modeling. Every time you watch the way a dog gives you attention, you can recommit yourself to being a more present, receptive, and selfless listener. The dog can be your ever-present inspiration to up your game.

If you are curious as to how many leash laws you are capable of breaking, try this simple experiment. The next time you're in a casual conversation, make a mental note of each time you: a) violate a leash law; b) are about to violate a leash law; c) are even for a fraction of a second thinking about violating a leash law. This means that every time you find yourself just waiting for your turn to speak, thinking of an "even better story" than the person speaking, daydreaming about Aspen, or having that sudden itch to interrupt, do something to draw attention to the infraction, like pinching your leg. Be honest and accountable. Now that you are self-aware, you might be surprised to find out how often you violate the leash laws.

The Rewards of Listening Like a Dog

Dogs work for rewards, so why wouldn't you? After all, without rewards, there's nothing to motivate you to learn the lessons of this book. Felt rewards are what motivate us to change habits and learn new skills.

Here are some real and immediate rewards you'll gain by learning to listen like a dog:

Powerful impressions. Listen like a dog and you *will* make a mark on others. Want to make an impression at a business convention or party? Don't be the scene stealer; be the "designated listener." *Everyone* will remember having talked to you, not because of what *you* said, but because of how you made *them* feel. The late American poet Maya Angelou once claimed, ". . . people will forget what you said, people will forget what you did, but people will never forget how you made them feel."

Likeability. We *like* people who listen to us. Listening skills alone will raise your likability status by several points on a ten-point scale. We will explore *likeability* further ahead.

Trust. Listening builds trust. Why? Because it shows people that you're genuinely open to input. If people know that you listen to them, and to others, they are much likelier to trust your decision making.

Knowledge. It's simple math: People who listen receive more information than those who never shut up. And knowledge is power. Smart businesspeople listen carefully to their customers, their competitors, their peers, and their front-line workers. Good listening allows you to get the real scoop.

Healing. Everyone has a need to be heard. The vast majority of tensions, conflicts, and impasses in business, politics, and personal life stem from people not feeling fully heard *or* making assumptions about others whom *they* have not fully heard. Listening is the cure. Listening, not just time, is what heals most wounds.

Unity. Nothing does more to cure divisiveness and tension in groups than listening. Listening can defuse dangerous or painful emotions. Understanding creates peace. A listening-intensive environment is safer and more productive than one in which "being right" is the main objective.

Buy-in. Team members, investors, bosses, and other stakeholders are *much* more likely to support your initiatives if they feel their input has been heard and incorporated. A customer is much more likely to buy from you if you have heard and understood his/her needs and concerns.

🦴

Ultimately, though, listening like a dog is its own reward. It enriches *your* relationships with the people around you, from your spouse and children, to your boss and coworkers, to the guy who runs the coffee truck. And that makes life more beautiful—plain and simple. Nothing creates a bond with another human being faster than listening to him/her. Nothing creates intimacy in a friendship, a marriage, or a family like listening does. All it takes is awareness and effort. (After all, not much of value comes free or easy.)

No one who makes the effort to learn to listen better ever says, "Geez, that was a waste of time. Wish I'd worked on my chip shot instead." *Everyone* who makes the effort experiences benefits—everyone.

Dogs know this intuitively. Humans need to be taught.

Something to
Chew On . . .

I always make YOU the star of the conversation, not me.

Watch the way *I* listen. Try to imitate my unselfish presence.

Everyone just wants to be understood—that's all that matters!

Danny, the READ Dog

Danny, a blue-and-white greyhound, was living a sad life, wandering the
streets of Cork, Ireland. Fortunately, he was rescued from an uncertain
fate and is now a celebrity among schoolchildren as he travels around
the United Kingdom providing a remarkable service. Now hear this:
Danny listens to schoolchildren read aloud. That's right, he *listens*. Danny
even has an official designation: READ (Reading Education Assistance
Dog) or, as the dogs are generally called in the UK, "listening dogs."

It seems many children find it easier to read aloud to a dog than
a human. Why? "When children read to him," reports an article in the
online London paper, *The Guardian*, "Danny does not criticise or correct
their pronunciation . . . '[This] helps with their self-esteem in reading out
loud because he is non-judgmental,' says the dog's owner. . . . 'He doesn't
judge them and he doesn't laugh at them. . . . The children don't realise
they are reading.'"[5]

Children like the idea of reading to dogs, especially because, in the
words of one student, "They don't answer back and they don't give you
a hard time."[6] Those who find it difficult to read are appreciative that
Danny might need to scratch his ear, and possibly even take a quick
nap—but he'll never roll his eyes or interrupt them if they take too long
or stumble over a word or two.

Danny has received much recognition and many awards, including
The International Fund for Animal Welfare (IFAW) Amazing Animal
award for his work as a listening dog.

---

5 *http://www.guardian.co.uk/education/2011/feb/28/dogs-listen-to-children-reading*
6 *http://www.librarydogs.com/UK-Danny.html*

TWO

Keep It "Fur" Real: Going Low-Tech

*One reason a dog can be such a comfort
when you're feeling blue is that he
doesn't try to find out why.*

—Author Unknown

You may still be intrigued to learn how Fido, sitting at your feet and furiously scratching that sudden itch attack, could possibly guide you to the personal prosperity Promised Land. Nevertheless, if you find yourself doubting the pawsibility of my thesis consider these questions:

Would a dog log on to eHydrants.com to post a profile instead of . . . um, "using" a real hydrant?

Would a dog spend its afternoons roaming around World of Woofcraft with a *virtual* dog pack instead of its real friends?

Would a dog *pretend* to listen to you because it was too busy tweeting (or arfing, as the case may be)?

If you asked a dog to go for a walk, would it look vaguely annoyed at you for interrupting its texting session and tell you to "Shoot me an e-mail with the deets"?

Would a dog sniff another dog's *virtual* butt instead of the real McCoy?

Technology today is a truly magical thing. It lets us communicate in all sorts of exciting ways that we couldn't just a few years ago—text messages, e-mail, Skype, GoToMeeting, Twitter, etc. It lets us summon help when our car breaks down in the desert and order a pizza while lying on the beach. It lets us schedule and reschedule meet-ups in real time. It lets us play Scrabble with a partner in Vancouver while sitting on our front porch in Albuquerque. It lets us share videos of dogs on skateboards with our circles of friends, and their friends, and the friends of the friends of their friends.

Few would argue that technology isn't pretty awesome, but . . .

It seems the easier, faster, and more fun it's becoming to connect with one another virtually, the harder it's becoming to connect with one another in reality. That's a loss. A biggie.

Here's where I think the heart of the problem lies: *listening* is where humans forge real and lasting connections with other people, but technology *drastically reduces our need and opportunity to truly listen.*

Techno-Primary Relationships

E very advance we make in virtual communications eliminates yet another need to connect in person. For example, each time you buy a product online, you forgo a trip to a brick-and-mortar store (where you typically have face-to-face conversations). This may be a good way to save time, but it also decreases our connections with other live human beings. Technology also reduces the number of live conversations you have with friends, colleagues, and relatives. Texts and e-mails have become primary ways to "talk" to others. Texting is great when it *facilitates* personal encounters ("Let's meet at Smitty's at 5"), but not so great when it *replaces* them.

Increasingly, our relationships with the people outside our immediate home or office are being reduced to techno-primary ones. Less and less often do we need to see these people in the flesh or talk to them live. As a loony example, someone dear to me told me that one of her best friends recently announced she needed to switch her relationships to primarily texting relationships. She said that with work and the kids, she no longer had time for talking on the phone, not to mention meeting in person with friends. Yep. Sad. Texting, social networking, e-mailing, and online games are seriously diluting the attention we pay to the people around us. I recently visited a family, and when I saw them sitting together in the living room, with no TV on, I thought, *Hurray for family time!* I quickly realized, though, that each of them was using an iPhone or iPad! Two were playing online games, one was instant-messaging, another was skimming her social networking sites. A family of four—or four strangers in the same room?

Interestingly, if you are a heavy techno-adopter, you may not *feel* you've lost touch with the human race. In fact, you probably believe you're *ultra*-connected. But consider how your relationships are becoming more digitized, abstract, and time-delayed. Thanks to e-mail, texting, and voicemail, you now respond to people at *your* convenience, rather than theirs, eliminating much of the need to *listen* to live human beings—and even when you do listen, you do so on your terms and your schedule.

The more real your smartphone and tablet are becoming to you, the more unreal *people* are becoming. Is that an overstatement? I wish it were. In the movie *Her*, a lonely, introverted, depressed man develops a love relationship with an intelligent computer operating system (OS), personified through a female voice. He becomes completely content with this "virtual" woman versus one in real life. The "virtual" woman was a great listener, however. Fascinating.

Listening is where humans forge real and lasting connections with other people, but technology *drastically reduces our need and opportunity to listen.*

Technology reduces our need and opportunity to listen.

Dogs, the Low-Tech Wonder

Dogs, however, are the real deal.

At a time when human relationships are becoming more abstract and virtual, dog ownership is at an all-time high. Coincidence? I suspect not.

Dogs are the one relationship in our lives that refuses to be digitized in any way. Dogs are the ultimate in low tech: a furry, warm, wet, "fragrant" presence in a circuitry-driven world.

Dogs are all about the real: the perfect antidote to our rushed, superficial, click-button style of communicating. In the midst of our digital world, dogs remain stubbornly *analog,* and that's what we love about them. Dogs insist upon being rolled around with and petted. You can't send a dog an e-mail or a text. (Well, you *can,* but it's generally not very productive.) Dogs demand our full, living presence.

Dogs tear us away from our computers and iPads. They get us dirty, wet, and smelly. They jump all over us and give us slobbery kisses. They inconvenience us tremendously—and we love them for it.

David Shaw, a psychologist on Maui, was recently quoted in a *New York Times* article as saying, "Today, dogs are one of the primary relationships—if not the primary relationship—in many people's lives."[7] Your dog is your lifeline to what's real.

What if *you* were to be that kind of presence to others? What if you refused to be digitized away? What if you were to risk being a slight inconvenience to others in exchange for being real and authentic?

Consider how that might affect your life and your career. How would that help you make your mark on the world?

As you consider your responses, let's take a look at some of the challenges of communicating in today's techno world.

Quality Versus Quantity

When it comes to communications, numbers are the new macho. We often take pride in the sheer *volume* of our LinkedIn connections, Twitter followers, and Facebook friends.

---

7 *http://www.nytimes.com/2014/07/20/magazine/is-your-relationship-with-fido-on-the-rocks.html*

Not long ago, LinkedIn sent out virtual "awards" to users who had hit the top 5 percent and top 1 percent of "most viewed profiles," designating these people as "Influencers." I saw some colleagues of mine earnestly congratulating one another on having attained one of these LinkedIn achievements.

But what do these numbers really mean? How many of your online "friends" would you know if you passed them on the street? How many could you call on the phone, knowing they'd drop what they were doing to give you a shoulder to cry on?

Does having hundreds of digital contacts provide us any real value?

Well, yes, in certain ways, it does. In business, for example, it can be helpful to have a large network, especially if you are selling a particular skill, product, or service, or are seeking to meet new people in your field. But my personal (and admittedly biased) observation is that many of us put a lot of effort into beefing up the *quantity* of our connections without gaining much *quality* in return. I mean, can we really maintain *relationships* with 632 people?

Not according to anthropologist Robin Dunbar. In a recent article in *IEEE Spectrum*, he asserts that, owing to the structure of our primate brains, the largest number of relationships we can handle is around 150. This is now known as the Dunbar number.

However, Dunbar also says, "If you start to invest less time in a friendship, the emotional quality of the relationship will decay within at most six months. The relationship will gradually bump its way down . . . until eventually it slips over the weir [dam] at 150 and that person becomes 'one of those people I once knew.'"[8]

---

8 *http://spectrum.ieee.org/telecom/internet/how-many-friends-can-you-really-have*

The true value of sites like Facebook, then, may be that they allow us to *tend* our real-world relationships, to keep them alive and relevant. That's great, provided we also do some connecting with these people *in* the real world. Otherwise, all we've succeeded in doing is juggling a greater number of pseudo relationships.

No self-respecting dog would stand (or sit, or stay) for that.

The Time Crunch

Another way that technology shrinks communication is by demanding that you do more with less time. So you are almost *forced* to make your communications faster, more efficient, and less personal. Every new technology that comes along is first seen as a way to save time. But, of course, it never does. The telephone was supposed to save us the time of traveling to meetings. E-mail was supposed to save us the time and delay of making phone calls and mailing letters. But what happens is that *everyone* adopts the technology and then we all just expect each other to get more done in the course of a day. No one would have expected an employee in the 1970s to write fifty letters a day, even if that was his or her entire job, but many people now routinely send that number of e-mails daily, *while* tending to many other important responsibilities. Naturally, this makes us eager to keep our communications brisk and no frills.

At some point you need to make a decision. Are you just going to play the digital efficiency game? Or, are you going to become a dog-like presence in the lives of others? Real. Messy. Attentive. Caring.

I urge you to consider making the sloppy, furry choice.

What's Lost Between the Digits

To "digitize" anything means to break it down into modular units. Think of a digital photo, for example. It creates a representation of a picture, but it's really just a collection of individual pixels. The more closely you look at it, the more you realize what's missing. Your brain fills in all the missing stuff.

Today, many of our communications are reduced to purely digital choices: to "like" someone's post or not; to "accept" a friend request or not; to rate a review as helpful or not.

You might think real information is being exchanged here, but is it? The shaded truth behind the digits becomes lost.

I can imagine the day in the near future, when communications are reduced to clicking icons or pre-written snatches of conversation:

RECEIVED: "Ellen has sent you a conversation module.
Would you like to accept? ☺ or ☹"
SENT: "☺"
RECEIVED: "Dear [Bob], I am breaking up with you. Good-
bye." (module created by ChatSplats, ©2019)
SENT: "☹"

The problem with digitization is that you end up not knowing people as well as you think. The biggest part of the other person is lost between the digits. You fill in the rest with your own mind and your own biases.

The funny thing is, we think we live in an advanced age of communications, but, because of digitization, much of our communication has been reduced to crude symbols that are wildly open to misinterpretation.

But the important stuff in life—the real, human stuff—is tender, shaded, and subtle. It doesn't come through in digital form. It has to be experienced *live*.

It has to get on your lap and lick you like a dog.

Text Wars

More and more, our communications are being channeled into text. We *love* texting. It's clean and efficient. Also, we don't feel as if we're bothering or inconveniencing others when we do it. Most of all, we're not inconveniencing ourselves. "Do I really need to call them? Can't I just shoot off a text?" It's funny to me how burdensome the phone call has become to so many people. Consider that when we text, we are sending a set of words to the receiver, and yet we're not considering that a large percentage of our communication comes through our tone, our body language, and ourselves. So that means, by texting we're leaving a lot of who we are on the cutting-room floor. That doesn't matter so much when we're exchanging factual information, but it matters a lot when we're talking about anything with an emotional component. And that's a lot of things.

By texting we're leaving a lot of who we are on the cutting-room floor.

Still, texting has become a preferred means of communicating in business—so much so that I now get a look of mild surprise when I ask someone to call me back. "*Call?* Can't I just shoot you a text?" It's like I've just asked them to send a letter by Pony Express. This shift is happening in our personal lives, too. I am shocked to observe, for example, how texting has overtaken the dating world. I recently witnessed a colleague of mine telling a woman he was dating that he'd like to call her that evening. Her reply? "Just text me." Understand: she wasn't blowing him off; in fact, she liked him! In the dating world, texting has far too often become *the* primary means of communication. A woman will leave her number for a man so he can *text her.* She gets excited when she receives a *text* from him, and feels hurt when she doesn't receive a text. A man will ask a woman out via text, ask about her day via text, tell her how pretty she is via text, and eventually break up with her via text (unless she texts him first for that same reason). It's a miracle people ever got together before text messaging came along.

Why do we favor texting so much these days? The short answer, I believe, is that when we communicate by text, we don't have to *listen.* We've trained ourselves not to listen! After all, who has time to listen?! Let's face it, we've become lazy, and a simple little text allows us to feel that we have done our part to communicate. Yay.

The dangerous part of texting is that we have the opportunity to insert our own interpretation of the text. When you receive a text, you receive a set of words that are up to you to guess the intent. Have you ever been involved in one of these mishaps? Someone texts something and it's taken differently than intended and then, uh oh—mayhem! The famous quote "The road to hell is paved with good intentions" comes to mind here. If the human element was present, we could avoid many of these mishaps, which occur at an astonishing rate.

It's fascinating that, even as texting has been gaining popularity, we have been inventing new technologies that can actually *improve* our ability to connect and listen: Skype and FaceTime, for example. If you had asked me twenty-five years ago which would be a more popular form of communicating in the future—video phone calls or written text—I would have guessed the former, hands down. But that hasn't happened. For most of us, text is king.

Why? I think one big reason is because Skype forces us to do many of the same things we have to do in live conversations. Not only do we have to comb our hair, clean our desks, and look presentable (no minor consideration), but we also have to *engage* with the other person. We have to make (virtual) eye contact and actually listen. We can't be sneakily writing e-mails or clipping our toenails. Sad but true.

Output, Output, Output

Another weakness of technology, from a connection standpoint, is that, as I mentioned earlier, it's caused us to fall in love with output, not input (i.e., listening).

The Internet lets us advertise ourselves without the inconvenience of giving reciprocal attention to someone else. Many people today, it seems, are looking for *followers* more than conversational part-ners. They want people to "like" their Facebook pages and read their tweets and blogs. It's totally one-way. No listening required.

We're coming dangerously close to the day we don't even tell our mates we love them anymore—"Just follow me on Instagram, honey."

To me, all of this output shows a desperate desire to be heard, and the Web lulls us into a false sense of being heard. Just because 759 people have seen your post doesn't mean you've been *listened* to—it means you've given 759 people a chance to offer *their* output in response to *your* output.

Dogs, on the other hand, are much more invested in receiving input—smells, sounds, sights—than they are in producing output (obvious poop jokes aside). A dog is in bliss when it can just lie there, smelling the scents and listening to the sounds being carried by the breeze. A walk in the woods is the greatest treat in the world for a dog. Because it's an opportunity to bark and make noise? No, because it's an opportunity to download all the glorious sensory input available there.

The Myth of Multitasking

One of the worst ways in which technology has weakened the art of listening has been to make multitasking the norm. Technology makes it possible to listen *while* doing other things—like posting a YouTube video—or so we tell ourselves.

The truth is that multitasking is an illusion. Humans *can't* actually multitask; we can focus on only one task at a time. Brain studies show that when we try to do two things at once, such as write an e-mail and have a conversation, *task interference* is created and our brains get scrambled. What we're really doing when we *think* we're multitasking is rapidly shifting our attention from one task to another.[9] We might believe we're listening to someone *while* writing a text message—"Yeah, yeah, I'm listening, go on"—but we're not. We're selectively tuning the person in and out, and of course losing much of what is being said. And the other person feels it.

The crazy thing is that we multitask in the name of efficiency, but we're really being extremely inefficient. We would get much more done if we just attended to one task at a time, fully and completely. That means if someone walks into our office to talk, it's better to stop writing that e-mail and actually *listen* to the person for a few minutes—and then return to the e-mail. In this way, we not only do a much better job of hearing the person, but we also write a better e-mail, in less time.

Dogs do one task at a time. When it's time to listen, that's *all* they do. And think about this: dogs have *much* more sensitive ears than ours, so theoretically they should be more easily distracted than we are; but their ability to focus on the task at hand and on the person they're with is amazing. We could learn a great deal about "uni-tasking" from dogs.

The Wonders of Low-Tech

If you want to influence people, you need to put the human touch back into your communications. Ironically, that means being more like a dog. It means offering your live, messy presence to others —in person if possible, by phone or Skype if not.

---

9 *http://www.npr.org/templates/story/story.php?storyId=95256794*

We get to know people best by seeing and hearing them in real time. That means that in today's tech-driven world, the best way to get noticed is to step outside the tech bubble and be real. I'm not saying you should *abandon* technology; just use it more consciously and deliberately. Each of the new tools at your disposal—texting, social networking, e-mail—has some great assets. Texting, for example, is terrific for making plans on the fly. Facebook is great, as I mentioned earlier, for *tending* relationships, provided there is something real being tended. When you need to quickly check a traffic report, thank goodness for the smartphone. A casual flirt? Fun! Arguing with a significant other via text? Not so much. Where we go wrong is when we use techno communications for purposes that require a human touch—or when we give them priority over a human who is actually present.

Ask yourself: will this lead to stronger real-world connection?

This is the bottom-line question you should ask yourself every time you techno-communicate: will this communication lead to a stronger *real-world* connection with this person, or am I using it as a *substitute* for a real-world connection? If the latter is true, make the low-tech choice.

I was in a car accident a few years ago and received many texts and e-mails wishing me well. Though I appreciated these messages—I really did—the one person who really *made a mark* on me was a friend who made the effort to call me several times to actually *ask* how I was doing and to *listen* to my answers. He didn't take over and tell me all about the accident that *he* was in eons ago and the peril he endured. The conversation was about *my* accident, not his. I felt heard. I felt cared about. No leash-law violations occurred, and I appreciated it.

If *you* want to make a mark, truly make a mark, try to avoid digital communication whenever possible. Pick up the phone and make a call. *Walk* over to someone's office and talk in person. Arrange a lunch or get-together. Handle awkward and difficult conversations personally, not by e-mail. Always respond to a phone call with a phone call, not a text. After all:

Would a dog *text* you a request for a treat, even if it could?
Would a dog click a "wag tail" button to tell you it liked you?
Would a dog wait in line for days for the release of the iBark 9?

When it comes to personal relationships, take a tip from your dog; try these low-tech, high-impact options:

- Go for a walk together
- Play
- Touch
- Spend some time together in a natural setting
- Hang out, with no agenda
- Most of all, listen—every chance you get.

Want to make a mark? Put the smartphone away. It'll still be there when you need it. Promise.

Something to
Chew On . . .

I'm a furry ball of low-tech fun and I am real; that's why you love me.

Listening—I mean *live* listening—is where real connections happen, folks.

Get your face out of that computer screen!

Pavlov's Dogs

If you've ever taken a psychology class, no doubt you studied the concept of "classical conditioning." This famous theory was conducted by Russian physiologist Ivan Pavlov, aided by his team of assistants—notably dogs. Pavlov was studying the response of salivation and the digestive system when he noticed that the dogs would often begin salivating even in the absence of food and smell. As he discovered, the dogs were reacting to lab coats because every time the dogs were served food, the person who served it was wearing a lab coat. Therefore, the dogs reacted as if food was on its way whenever they saw a lab coat.

In a series of experiments, Pavlov then tried to figure out how these phenomena were linked. For example, he struck a bell at doggie dinnertime. If the bell was sounded in close association with their kibble, the dogs learned to associate the sound of the bell with food. Subsequently, at the mere sound of the bell, they responded by drooling. This response is called "conditioned reflex," and the process whereby dogs or humans learn to connect a stimulus to a reflex is called "conditioning."

The experiences of Pavlov and his intrepid team of canines can also teach us how thoroughly conditioned we are, especially when listening. We hear a word that triggers an emotional response—like "taxes"—and suddenly we're off in our own world, worrying about our 1040 and no longer effectively listening. Once we recognize our own leash-law violations, we can take control and come back into the conversation—fully present and attentive.

THREE

Listen with Your Whole Being

When humans are sad or unhappy,
silent companionship is the order of the day.
. . . That usually cheers them up.

—Bob (the West Highland Terrier),
A Dog's Guide to Humans by Karen Davison

Dogs have amazing ears, *much* better than ours. Not only can their ears be moved independently to "catch" sound and pinpoint its exact source(s), but they can also detect much higher frequencies than ours and, according to Dog Breed Info Center, hear sounds from about four times farther away than human ears.[10]

That explains why dogs are such great listeners, right? Well, no, not entirely. Sure, great hearing is part of the equation, but the reason dogs are such great listeners—*especially to humans*—is that they don't *just* listen with their ears, they listen with their *whole being.* Dogs know instinctively, if not intellectually, that listening goes far beyond merely snagging sound waves from the air.

To truly listen—like a dog—means to give someone your undiluted, committed, and fully energized attention. That kind of attention requires much more than an opening of the ears; it requires a

---

10 *http://www.dogbreedinfo.com/articles/dogsenses.htm*

whole body/whole being commitment. That's what dogs give to us. And this experience we humans have—of feeling *paid attention to* by dogs—is not just wishful thinking on the part of dog lovers. As it turns out, there's a growing body of scientific work suggesting that dogs, of all the creatures in the animal kingdom (including our closest cousins, the great apes), are tuned in to us as no other being on Earth is. This is probably a function of their intelligence, combined with their almost total dependence on us for food, shelter, and ball-throwing. But whatever the explanation, dogs seem to have made a collective decision to *zero in* on humankind with such laser-like focus that they almost seem to be reading our minds. This deep connection dogs have with us seems to go back thousands of years in our collective history.

In her wonderful book *Inside of a Dog: What Dogs See, Smell, and Know*, Alexandra Horowitz goes into fascinating detail about the ways dogs pay attention to us. Dogs study the daily activities we engage in. They study the way we walk and move. They study our facial expressions (a *lot*, and with an ultra-fine degree of discernment). They study our habits and the *breaking* of our habits. They study our schedules. They study our posture, body language, and energy levels. They sniff out changes in our body chemistry. They study our moods and intentions. They even study what *we* study— dogs, it seems, are experts at knowing where *our* attention is focused and then responding to that. All it takes is the subtlest change in our attention, or *in*tention, and dogs know where our interest has shifted. For example, just *try* entertaining the thought *Think I'll take the dog for a walk* and hiding those intentions from your dog. (Good luck with that, by the way.)

Attention = Energy

By contrast, we humans aren't very good at paying attention to one another. We might notice if someone's arm falls off (provided we're not getting a text message at the time), but we don't pay much attention to the finer details. Honed, focused attention is really what listening like a dog is all about. When a dog pays attention to a human, it pulls out all the stops. It uses its eyes, its nose, it ears, its tactile senses—its entire energy system.

What are some of the ways we can tell if a dog is listening to us?

- Sitting up alertly
- Cocking its head
- Moving its ears
- Looking us in the eye (that amazing canine *gaze*)
- Moving physically closer to us
- Touching (such as laying a paw on our foot)
- Licking
- Moving the tail or holding it up
- Muscle alertness
- "Working" its nose in our direction
- And most important:
- Keeping its mouth closed (no barking, growling, or whining)

There's none of that "Are you listening to me?" stuff that humans are always asking each other; there's no mistaking a dog's attention. Of course, we humans don't have tails, dynamic noses, or expressively moving ears, but we do have our own dandy set of human faculties that can be quite effective in the attention-paying game. We just need to use them. The point is, attention is an *active* form of energy, not a passive one. It's something we literally *beam out*. "Whole being" listening is a state in which all of your energy, not just your hearing sense, is directed toward the other person. It's about tapping into your inner dog. Most of us experience this heightened kind of listening only once in a while. But we can make it a replicable experience by using the following three keys.

> 1. **Make the commitment to listen.**
> 2. **Listen with your eyes, heart, and ears.**
> 3. **Let your attention show in your whole body.**

Making the Commitment to Listen

The main reason most of us fail as listeners is that we approach listening in a lazy, undisciplined, and decidedly non-doggy way. We fail to make the commitment to listen. You must make a *conscious and deliberate decision* to disengage from whatever mode you're currently in—speaking mode, daydreaming mode, writing mode, game mode, zoning out to *So You Think You Can Dance* mode— and devote yourself, whether for ten seconds or two hours, to pure, focused listening.

You must make this commitment prior to entering any situation where listening is going to be your role. But you should also make it on an as-needed basis many times over the course of a day. As soon as you see that someone needs your listening attention and you decide to give it, you must make the commitment to listen and actively shift gears into listening mode. If you don't make the commitment, your attention remains split and diffused.

The commitment to listen really is as simple as commanding yourself: "STOP current mental activity; shift into listening gear." It can help to actually envision a stop sign in your mind or to imagine the sound of a buzzer (psychologists call this process "thought-stopping"). On the other hand, it isn't always so simple in practice. Our minds, by nature, are complicated and full of noise, thus we tend to zone out. We almost need a traffic cop in our heads directing things since it's so congested in there. Making the commitment to listen is an incredibly respectful thing to do, however. It communicates: you are more important to me than my need to . . . finish this e-mail right now; make this brilliant Scrabble play on my iPad; or get this onion chopped. It also leads to efficiency and goodwill, because (1) you hear the person's message without asking to have it repeated five times; (2) the other person feels heard and validated; and (3) you can then go back to what you were doing before with 100 percent of your attention. Everyone wins!

Dogs do this naturally. They don't give you half-baked attention while trying to chew a bone—"Yeah, yeah, I'm listening; go on." They may be 100 percent wrapped up in that bone, but when they notice you talking to them, and they make the commitment to listen, their

If you want someone to listen, ask if it's a good time.

head pops up and they leave the bone behind. They switch 100 percent of their attention to you. Then, when you're finished addressing them, they go back to giving 100 percent of their attention to the bone.

If you want someone to listen to you—really listen—first ask them if it's a good time for them to listen. It's a mistake to assume that whenever we want to talk, the other person is ready to listen like a dog. The truth is that *they* have distractions, moods, and time constraints that may make it challenging for them to fully take us in at that moment. By gaining *their* commitment to listen, not only are we gaining their respect for asking, but we're more likely to get a doglike listener (when they're ready).

The most important part of the commitment to listen is to turn on your three main listening receptors: your eyes, your heart, and your ears.

The Eyes Have It

Ask people what the most important organ for listening is and ten out of ten of them will say the ears. And while it's true that we collect much of our verbal information through the ears, it's also true that our ears are virtually useless in making connections with fellow human beings.

Human ears just sit there, looking like some weird species of mollusk we wouldn't eat if we found it in a bowl of paella. They funnel sound waves, but they communicate absolutely no emotion; they have almost no expressive power whatsoever; they are completely passive organs.

Here's where dogs have us beat. Dogs' ears *are* expressive. They not only move about, individually, to track sound, but they also perk up when the dog is excited, go askew when the dog is confused, droop when the dog is sad (or busted from getting into the trash again), and go flat when the dog is angry. A dog has at least eighteen separate muscles that control its ear movements.[11]

So how can we humans compensate for our decidedly non-expressive ears? By using our eyes.

Your eyes are the most overlooked and underrated listening apparatus you possess. The eyes are *extremely* powerful instruments of connectivity for humans, but they are rarely treated with the level of importance they deserve. Sure, you may hear advice like, "Don't forget to make good eye contact . . . oh, and wear a red power tie, too" in communications workshops, but that's about as far as it goes. If you want to become a better connecter, though, you must learn to use your eyes as the power tools they are. And once again, dogs have a lot to teach us.

Even if dogs could not use their ears so expressively, they would still be models of intense listening because of the power of their gaze. The canine gaze is legendary in its purity and focus. Many people have argued about whether a dog has a "soul" or is capable of emotions similar to ours. For dog lovers, the question is cleared up easily: just look into a dog's eyes.

---

11 *http://thebark.com/content/amazing-facts-about-dogs-ears*

The living presence that is seen through one's eyes—human or canine—cannot be faked. In the eyes you see the very center of awareness, the operator of the biological hardware, the captain of the ship. In the eyes you see emotional truth.

Want to hook someone emotionally? Show them a picture of a child or an animal making eye contact with the camera. Want to make an instant connection with a stranger? Look him or her in the eye. Want to engage someone's help and cooperation? Make eye contact.

Conversely, want to *avoid* engagement? Avoid being chosen as a volunteer? Avoid helping another person? Look away. (This doesn't always work. Teachers know the technique so well they often deliberately pick the kid who looks away. And, of course, when you come home and your dog won't look you in the eye, you know there's a mess somewhere, right?)

A focused gaze communicates sincerity, conviction, and basic human connection. That's why looking away is often seen as a sign of deceit. When Richard M. Nixon lost the 1960 presidential election, many attributed it to his habit of shifting his eyes during the nation's first-ever televised debate. Similarly, the infamous "thousand-yard stare" of traumatized war veterans and victims signals *dis*connection —from others, with that unfocused and blank stare.

But the eyes are more than just windows; they may, in fact, be closer to *lasers*, capable of *beaming out* energy and information. Many cultures throughout history have believed this. Belief in the evil eye, for example—the ability of a focused stare to cause harm to another person—has been widespread throughout the world. We know it as a mother to the teenager who took the car without permission, a wife to a husband who was caught with a hand in the cookie jar, so to speak, one boxer to the other in the ring, Predator versus Alien, you get the gist of it. Also common is the belief that humans can control, enlighten, hypnotize, and heal other people simply by the power of their gaze. Interestingly, some belief systems, such as Zoroastrianism, have attributed this type of power to dogs as well![12]

Western science, of course, rejected this "primitive" idea that the eyes are capable of emitting energy (extramission theory) long ago when it adopted the model of the eye as basically a biological Nikon. Some scientists today, however, are taking another look and, once again, discovering truth in ancient wisdom.

Scientist Rupert Sheldrake, for example, became fascinated by the common feeling that one is being watched. Why do we so often seem to know when someone is staring at us? Is the phenomenon real or just our imagination? (Any guy who has tried to steal a long look at a beautiful woman knows it's real. He gets caught every time.) In his book *The Sense of Being Stared At and Other Unexplained Powers of Human Minds*, Sheldrake describes interviews with numerous people who watch others for a living: police officers, detectives, security guards, and surveillance personnel. Most of them, through experience, are convinced that people can, in fact, tell when they're being watched. He also cites several experiments that strongly indicate that humans can indeed detect the stare of an unseen stranger. Private investigators, writes Sheldrake, know this phenomenon so well they actually learn methods for avoiding triggering their subjects' "stare detectors."

---

12 *http://tenets.zoroastrianism.com/dog33.html*

Dr. Colin A. Ross has taken it a step further and developed a device that can measure energy coming from an open eye. He has detected measurable "brain wave" emissions coming from the human eye, and has also found that the intensity of this emitted energy changes with the brain's activity (suggesting that the looker's mental *intentions* can have a significant effect on the beamed waves). Ross has patented a technology by which he hopes one day can create things like switches that can be turned on and off simply by looking at them. Imagine the "remote control wars" that will cause in family rooms everywhere!

Here are a few of the things that can be communicated to someone by making or maintaining eye contact:

- **Interest.** Looking at someone is the universal language for "You've got my attention."
- **Bonding.** If you want to make a connection with a person in a crowd or across a table, eye contact is the universal way.
- **Attraction.** To look at someone for longer than a couple of seconds is a way of showing *special* interest.
- **Encouragement to keep talking.** Making periodic eye contact means, "Go on, I'm interested in hearing more."
- **Intimidation.** Eye contact can also be used to dominate others, threaten them, warn them, or establish power over them.
- **Hierarchy.** Along similar lines, a social rule says that those with higher social, business, or political status may look directly into the eyes of those with lower standing, but not vice versa.
- **Attention.** Making eye contact with a person is a silent way of saying, *"Psst,* hey, over here."

- **Understanding.** Want to share an unspoken joke or communicate an "in the know" kind of understanding? Eye contact is the way.
- **Sincerity.** Unbroken eye contact communicates, "I am being sincere and honest; I can be trusted."
- **Confidence.** The ability to establish and hold eye contact is also a demonstration of self-esteem and self-belief. A confident person "looks you in the eye."
- **Love.** Nothing says, "I love you" like a long, intimate gaze.

Conversely, *breaking* eye contact or averting the eyes serves a great many purposes as well:

- Indicating embarrassment, shame, or sadness;
- Saying, "You're losing me. I'm ready to move on to a new topic";
- Attempting to avoid helping someone;
- Communicating the message, "You are not worth my attention";
- Cutting off or avoiding personal intimacy;
- Deferring to someone in a greater power position;
- Shifting into an internal thinking mode;
- Gaining social comfort and reducing conversational intensity.

Because eye contact has so much power and so many different meanings, both positive and negative, it is a difficult skill for many people to master. If you don't make enough eye contact, people may think you are shy, a dweeb, insincere, bored, insecure, or inaccessible. If you make too much eye contact, people may think you are creepy, intense, socially awkward, or domineering. No one wants to be thought of as a starer. It's all about balance.

As a model for good eye contact, it's hard to do better than dogs. They are naturally amazing at it. They gaze deeply, sincerely, and unselfconsciously, but they also know enough not to gaze too long—that at a certain point a gaze can become a threat or a challenge. Have you ever had a staring contest with a dog? Who won? If the answer is you, I will question whether or not you were cheating. Dogs will typically win, paws down, unless and until the UPS truck goes by or an SIA (Sudden Itch Attack) comes on.

Generally speaking, holding eye contact for four or five seconds at a time is good. It needn't be done more than half the total time you are talking to someone. In fact, eye contact for more than two-thirds of the time begins to indicate that you're hot for the person, which may not be your desired effect—especially if you're in the middle of an IRS audit.

The important thing is not about specific "rules," but rather to become aware of how you use your eyes and to know how powerful they are. Your eyes are the number-one way by which you establish connection with others and by which they gauge and assess you. The eyes are indeed the windows to your soul, so break out the Windex and turn up the inner lights.

Your Heart Has Ears

The second key organ of listening is the heart. Many of us, when listening, make the mistake of using only our heads. We focus all of our attention on trying to download the *information* that's being conveyed. But if you want to make a *connection*—the way a dog would—you need to engage with the *person* as well. That means using the heart.

As an organ of connection, the heart is every bit as important as the eyes. "Listen with your heart" might sound annoyingly touchy-feely, but it is critical advice in this era of Emotional Intelligence. You need to attune yourself emotionally to the people you're listening to—especially

As an organ of connection, the heart is as important as the eyes.

if you want to build any kind of lasting relationship, business or personal. Emotional attunement happens through the heart.

This has long been known by poets and songwriters, but science has always remained skeptical—until recently. A whole spate of new research is confirming that the heart is much more than a sophisticated pump. The heart, we are beginning to learn, actually feeds more electrical signals to the brain than the brain does to the heart, giving it a more primary role than we ever imagined. And these heart signals change under different emotional conditions, ordering the brain to function differently. When feeling stress, for example, the heart beats in a ragged pattern that cues the brain to shut down some of its higher thinking functions and go into survival mode. When feeling peaceful, loving, and positive emotions, the heart beats in a smoother and more orderly way (called *coherence*). This, in turn, calms the brain's emotional centers and allows our thought processes to be more relaxed, focused, clear, and efficient. The brain and the heart are in constant communication, and much of it is on an emotional level.[13]

What's perhaps most interesting, from a communications standpoint, is that scientists now know that the heart emits a powerful electromagnetic field. The heart's field is by far the most powerful magnetic field in the human body, about 5,000 times more powerful than the field emitted by the brain.[14] And this field is not *restricted to the body*; it radiates outward as far as ten feet away, where it can affect the hearts and brains of others. The really fascinating aspect of this, according to Rollin McCraty, PhD, Executive VP and Director of Research for the Institute of HeartMath, is that specific emotions are *encoded* within the electromagnetic field that the heart generates.[15] That means that we literally beam our emotional state out into the world. Ever wonder why some people, by their very presence, seem to lift us up and inspire us, while others seem to drain our energy like a psychic sump pump? For the first time in history, we have solid scientific evidence that our inner emotional state can permeate those around us.

What this means is that the heart absolutely cannot be left out of the listening equation. It must be factored in, and not only by therapists, poets, and energy healers, but also by salespeople and managers, friends and lovers.

To me, this comes down to a simple practice. To the extent you are capable, hold a caring feeling in your heart each time you enter into a listening encounter. Just hold that state and feel it in your

---

13 *www.heartmath.org/programs/emwave-self-regulation-technology-theoretical-basis/*

14 *http://www.wakingtimes.com/2012/09/12/the-heart-has-its-own-brain-and-consciousness/*

15 *https://www.youtube.com/watch?v=UxOd4YAk00Y*

chest. But also remember that your heart is a "tuner"—a receiver—as well as a sender. So keep a sense of openness and receptivity in your heart. This will allow you to tune in to some of the feelings of the other person as well. When that person says, or feels, something that touches you emotionally, allow yourself to feel it in *your* heart. Allow it to come through your eyes as well. Just quietly let the emotion register within you. The connection you form by resonating with the other person in this way will be a lasting and genuine one, even if there are superficial things you disagree about.

This might sound like New Age fluff to you, but I guarantee you that if you make a serious effort to begin listening with both your eyes and heart—again, there's no better model than a hound—you will notice a profound change in the way others respond to you. You will notice more trust, more affection, more sharing, more gratitude—and more willingness to involve you in high-level decision making. I've never heard a dog accused of being heartless. They're all heart, all of the time, and, in turn, we have love and affection in our hearts for them.

Listen with Your Ears

Of course, you need to listen with your ears as well. The problem for many of us is that we are unable to listen effectively with our ears because we are torn between listening to the flesh-and-blood person speaking *over there* and to the little person speaking to us *inside our head*. When you listen, you are often listening to both voices—the voice of the person speaking and the nonstop voice track that's yammering inside your own noggin.

The inner voice track is full of all sorts of worries and concerns: trying to think of a clever line to say, fretting about time and schedule issues, worrying about whether the conversation is tipping in your favor, trying to second-guess what the other person is going to say next, and even wondering what you're going to have for dinner. The result: the real person speaking to you fades into background noise, or, at best, gets a costarring role. How many times have you been "listening" to someone and you suddenly realize you have no clue what they just said to you? The reason? Your inner voice track began giving a command performance.

A huge part of the commitment to listen is making a conscious decision to turn down (or *off*, if possible) the inner voice track and turn up your actual ears. The key to a successful communicative experience is when there is only one voice speaking at a time. This includes inner and outer voices. It's amazing how much you can take in if you give total attention to what's coming in through your ears.

The key to successful communication: one voice speaking at a time.

Let Your Attention Show in Your Whole Body

The final challenge in listening with your whole being is to allow your whole body to participate in the listening process, by physically acknowledging what you hear. Notice I said, "allow," not "force."

As I mentioned earlier, there's never a doubt as to whether a dog is paying attention to you. Their entire body is involved—ears, eyes, head, nose, tail, limbs. You *know* you have their attention. It's indisputable. With human listeners, though, you're rarely so sure. Are they really listening or not? Most humans are somewhat inhibited in their body language and don't realize the importance of letting others *see* their attention and interest.

The fact is, no matter how fascinated you are with what's being said to you, it does little good if the person talking can't tell. So, part of great listening is learning to: (1) show attention through body alertness; and (2) respond in physical ways to what the speaker is saying (and feeling).

This does not mean trotting out a bunch of hammy behaviors like a bad actor. It means being physically responsive to the speaker in a way that feels comfortable and authentic to you. Perhaps you feel natural using enthusiastic facial expressions. Perhaps your comfort zone tends toward the more reserved. Perhaps you naturally show interest by nodding, or perhaps you tilt your head the way a listening dog does. Perhaps you're an easy laugher, perhaps not. Whatever feels true and authentic to you will come across as authentic to others. On the other hand, putting on expressions that aren't authentically yours will feel phony, both to yourself and others. The point is: *allow* physical expression to happen, and to happen in your own natural way.

Of course, you don't necessarily want to project *every* feeling you feel. Suspicion, boredom, or contempt for your boss may not be in your best interest to reveal. But when an emotion that is both honest and productive strikes you, allow it to play out physically in your body as well as in your heart and your eyes. Be generous enough to get your body into the act.

I say "generous" because physical feedback really is a gift to the person who's speaking. Dogs don't disguise or hide their enthusiasm and attention. You see it in every muscle in their body. Contrary to the famous painting, dogs would make lousy poker players. Humans don't realize the importance of bodily expression.

Learning to get your body into the act might take a little practice. It is more a matter of *releasing inhibitions* than teaching yourself a new skill. It is learning to *allow* your body to reflect what you're authentically feeling inside.

You might occasionally need to fake it a little. That's right: you might occasionally need to use the body language without feeling the feeling. I realize this goes against everything I've been saying about authenticity, but here's the interesting thing: if you use body language that is authentically *yours*, it often triggers the very emotional state you're emulating, and soon you're not faking it any longer; you're feeling it. (If you don't believe me, try smiling *your* signature smile. Admit it, you suddenly feel happier, don't you?)

Your ears, your eyes, and your heart, together, make up an incredibly powerful listener. The greatest challenge, though, is remembering to use them consciously and mindfully. This is where the commitment to listen comes in. Each time you begin to listen, even for just a minute, remind yourself to turn on your eyes, tune in your heart, open your ears, and bring your body into play. This is "whole being" listening—this is listening like a dog.

Something to

Chew On ...

Listen like I do—with your eyes, your heart, and your ears.

Pay attention to the important *person* sitting across the table from you—and turn down the voice inside your head.

Use your body to let people know you heard what they said. Wag your tail like me.

Mancs

If you visit the Hungarian town of Miskolc, you will find a statue of a
German shepherd near the Szinva stream and public square. The statue
was cast by sculptor Borbála Szanyi and erected in December 2004. The
beautiful and touching memorial honors a famous rescue dog named
Mancs ("paw"), who was a member of the Spider Special Rescue Team
based in Miskolc.

Mancs and the rescue team traveled around the world to search for
survivors after earthquakes. Mancs, who was known for his keen sense
of hearing and smell, could locate people trapped deep beneath the
earthquake rubble. As if this feat wasn't astonishing enough, he could
also differentiate whether the person was dead or alive, then indicate
his discovery with a very clear signal to the other members of the
rescue crew. If he sensed a deceased person, he laid down; when he
sensed someone alive beneath the rubble, he stood up, wagged his tail,
and barked.

Mancs and his owner, László Lehóczki, took part in several earthquake
rescue missions, including the 2001 earthquakes in El Salvador and India.
Mancs became famous worldwide when he helped rescue a three-year-
old girl who spent eighty-two hours under the ruins after the Izmit
(Turkey) earthquake of 1999. Sadly, Mancs passed away from pneumonia
on October 22, 2006. In honor of the dog and his heroic rescue efforts,
a feature film entitled *Mancs* (released internationally as *Paw*) was
released in late 2014, making a posthumous film star of the dog who
used his keen hearing and sense of smell to save lives.

FOUR

Sniff Around

The real hero here is God,
for blessing me with this nose and a
few other amazing appendages.

—Brian Griffin (the dog),
Family Guy, created by Seth MacFarlane

"Hi there, how are you?"

How many times a day do you hear variations of that question?

"How's it going?"

"How ya doin'?"

"What's shakin'?"

"How's it hanging?"

"What's new?" Or that peculiarly male version, *Whassup?*—often shortened to *'Sup?* and asked while the body is in full stride, without the asker even slowing down to *pretend* to hear the answer.

How many times a day do *you* ask that same kind of question?

Are you *really* looking for an answer when you ask these throwaway questions? Usually, I'm afraid, we're looking for and expect a throwaway response that allows us to *avoid* getting into a conversation and just get down to business. No interest in true connection, just get in, get out. Half the time the answer doesn't even match the question asked. You've been there, right? Someone says, "hi" and you reply, "Good, good," or "Not too bad." Your face turns slightly crimson. Not because you gave an empty, meaningless response, but because you gave the *wrong* empty, meaningless response. Thankfully, the other person probably didn't even notice. Why? Because he or she wasn't really listening to your answer to begin with.

The "Good, Good" Syndrome

When I'm giving a talk, I often start by asking the group the standard, "How are you?"

In response, the group predictably answers, "Good" in a less-than-effervescent tone.

I then say, "No, I asked 'How *are* you?'"

Unfailingly, the group shouts, "Good" in a louder, slightly more jacked-up voice.

They assume I'm playing the "I can't hear you" game. I tell them, "I didn't ask you to repeat your answer in a louder voice because I couldn't hear you, I asked how you *are*. Because I really want to know. Let me try again . . . how are you?"

At this point a few participants will mumble tentative responses, a few will shrug noncommittally, and the rest stare intently at their shoes. The truth is that a lot of my listeners aren't "good" at all. Some are tired, some are stressed out—no, many are—some of them are having problems at home and some may even be hung over.

"Good" is a pretty empty word, isn't it? It's a generic, all-purpose response. It usually means absolutely nothing. You might as well say "potato" instead. But that's the very purpose of "good," isn't it? To *be* meaningless. To *avoid* genuineness.

In fact, that's the purpose of much of today's "casual" conversation. It is not designed to build bridges between people, but to build *walls*. And to lubricate business transactions. After all, you can't just walk up to someone and ask, "How many widgets do you want to buy today?" So you throw out a "filler" question like "How's it going?"—not because you want to hear the answer, but because you need to say *something* to get things rolling.

I once heard the British playwright Harold Pinter say that the everyday purpose of language is not to communicate but to avoid communication. I thought he was just being a wiseass, but I've come to realize he was more than a little right.

It's an odd idea, isn't it. That language, our essential tool of communication, might be used to wall us off from one another, rather than to bring us closer? But that's exactly what much of language does. We use it to keep people at arm's length. But by shutting ourselves off from the possibility of real encounters with people, aren't we giving up a lot of what makes life meaningful and rewarding?

Homo Sapiens, the Great Communicator

I am fascinated by the language of casual encounters. I believe the way people handle casual communications is a reflection of the way they handle *all* communications.

We humans are "allegedly" the master communicators of the animal kingdom. Scientists say that language is *the* essential way humans differentiate themselves from the "lower" creatures. Our brains are structured, to a large extent, for just this purpose. Humans alone (supposedly) possess the ability to communicate abstract ideas, learn the intimate details of one another's lives, and express our thoughts and feelings in both precise and poetic ways.

Then why do we leave this miraculous tool in our pockets so much of the time? It's as if we're all gifted pianists who insist on playing "Chopsticks." We *can* communicate brilliantly, but instead we use words to put up façades, to hide, to mislead each other, to redirect each other, and to avoid the risk of real connection.

And yet we wonder why there is so much loneliness, alienation, and misunderstanding in our world.

Canis Familiaris, the Great Sniffer

Dogs, on the other hand, are supposedly our evolutionary inferiors due to their lack of words. As communicators, they take a distant backseat to humans. Or so we think. But look at how dogs handle even the most casual encounter.

Two dogs meet. They immediately "sniff each other out." They don't sniff superficially, either. They don't ask each other, from a polite distance, "How do you smell today?" and then answer "Good, good" in a falsely bright bark. Nah, they dive right for the most intimate parts of each other's anatomies and start sniffing.

Dogs, as you probably know, have an astonishing sense of smell, often estimated to be anywhere from a thousand to *10 million* times more powerful than that of humans.[16] A dog's brain is designed primarily to process smell. When a dog sniffs, it is downloading *reams* of information not available to the noses of mere mortals.

Just a small sampling of the things a dog learns by sniffing another dog:

- What that dog's been eating lately
- Where it's been hanging around the last few days, and the order of the places it has visited
- How relaxed and friendly it is
- How sexually active and interested it is
- Whether it's pregnant or not
- How healthy it is; whether it's carrying major illnesses
- What dead things it likes to roll in
- What other animals it lives with and near
- Who the hot hounds in the neighborhood are
- Whether it lives with a human family or not, and the make-up of that family
- And a thousand other things you can't even begin to imagine

A dog's nose is a story-gathering machine. In a very real sense, a dog listens with its nose—intently. When two dogs meet, something *real* happens between them. They encounter one another directly and intimately. They each make the other dog the most important thing in their universe, at least for that minute or two. They don't

---

16 *http://www.dogbreedinfo.com/articles/dogsenses.htm*

rush through the exchange, distracted by the goals they need to accomplish that day. They give the encounter their full presence and attention. They come to an understanding of each other.

Think, on the other hand, about the familiar scenario of two human dog walkers meeting each other on the street. While their two dogs are busily learning intimate details about each other's lives, the two humans are busily smiling superficially and saying, "Looks like rain." "Yep, sure does." Yet the two humans walk away from the encounter, confident in their status as great communicators.

For dogs, sniffing one another out is an *adventure*, a doorway to new worlds. Admittedly, that's because they have such amazing noses; sniffing is their mutant superpower. But you have a mutant superpower, too. It's your ability to ask questions and *listen* to answers. That's *your* doorway to new worlds.

Your ability to ask questions and listen to answers are your doorway to new worlds.

Remember the old cartoons, when a character would draw a door in the air and step right through it? The character would then emerge in an alternate universe—outer space, the Old West, or King Arthur's England. That's the power you have in your hands every time you enter an exchange with another human being. You can create a door to another universe. But most of the time you don't use that power. You don't make that other human being important enough to learn about. Your busy agenda takes precedence.

What would happen if you took a page from Dog's book? What if you took the opportunity—not with every single person you met, of course, but even just once or twice a day—to "sniff one another out"? I don't mean to *literally* sniff, because that might lead to things like restraining orders, but to do so in the poetic sense.

Try this. The next time you're in line at the grocery store, talk to someone: the person next to you or the clerk. You might find out the checkout clerk is new to the area. You might find the person in line behind you has a recipe for banana bread worth sharing, or a daughter about to graduate. Before you know it, you've widened the circle of people you know, even just a little.

On that long ride to the airport shared in a cab with a colleague, do a little asking, but more important, listen. You might just experience that warm, tail-wagging glow your dog knows about.

Take the Sniff Test

I'm sometimes a troublemaker; it's just my nature. For the past few years, I've been conducting an informal experiment. Almost every day, at least once or twice, I will take a casual exchange, like buying groceries, and try to turn it into a sniffing session. Sometimes I play the sniffer, sometimes I play the sniffee. Admittedly, this doesn't always go smoothly (sometimes people don't want to be "sniffed" and we need to respect that). But I usually make a mark: I forge a connection with a new person, and that changes the person's perception of me *from the generic to the specific*. I'll give you a few examples:

I recently stepped into an elevator and this guy was standing there. He said the typical, "How's it going?" thing, then snapped his eyes toward the floor-numbers display (notice he "said" and not "asked"). My first impulse was to toss out a typical conversation-ending "Good, good," but instead I confessed, "Well, I was doing good, but my favorite hockey team got hammered last night in a playoff game, so now I'm on life support." He gave a polite laugh, but I could see low-level panic creeping onto his face: *What have I gotten myself into?* I chatted a bit more about hockey, as he began staring at the elevator doors, *willing* them to open between floors, presumably so he could dive out into the empty shaft. As soon as the doors did open, he dashed out. Probably on the wrong floor.

Oh well, chalk one up in the loss column for me. No big deal. Interestingly, though, I ran into the same guy in the lobby a few days later and he made an effort to catch *my* attention. "Still watching hockey?" he asked with a smile. "I saw there was a game on last night" he added. It was a small thing, but it made me realize, by golly, I had made a mark with him. A small one, admittedly, but at least it was something—a specific connection. I'm probably known as "that hockey guy" to him. Still, next time we meet in an elevator, we'll have a starting point to build from.

In another elevator encounter, I ran into a sales rep from my company whom I had encountered professionally but didn't know personally. I gave her the old "How are you?" and received the expected chorus of "Good, good." I decided to sniff a bit more and asked "Good *good?*" She then admitted to me she was actually dreading a professional meeting with a doctor later that day. I asked her why.

She told me. I happened to know the doctor she would be meeting with and offered some advice that turned out to be just the thing she needed to give her some direction for the meeting. It was a brief conversation, but it had substance.

The end result? It felt productive to have a valuable exchange with a colleague that turned out to be helpful. The rep felt great to have been listened to and to *get* some good advice. And we both forged the beginnings of a possible friendship. The doctor, too, probably ended up benefitting from our exchange.

In a third example, I was recently dining out with some friends. When the server came over, we exchanged the usual round of "Good, good," then I asked how she *really* was. She seemed pleasantly surprised and thanked me for asking. I reassured her, "You are our lifeline to food, so how you're doing is very important to us." She laughed and told us she was in a good mood because her boyfriend had finally cleaned the apartment, something he'd been promising to do for ages. This seemed very important to her. It also prompted a lively five-way conversation for a couple of minutes, and suddenly she wasn't just our server anymore; she was our friend. She gave us special treatment for the rest of the evening, even slipped us a free dessert. We gave her a great tip. Everybody won.

People want to be heard.

Sniffing Pays

Those are just some very recent examples of the hundreds of rewarding experiences I've had over the past few years (in addition to a few rolled eyes) as a result of "sniffing" like a dog. Of course, not every exchange with every cab driver needs to be turned into Sunday with Oprah. Sometimes you just need to accomplish a task. Sometimes the "vibe" just isn't right.

But I do suggest that at least once or twice a day, in a situation where you would normally start mindlessly chirping, "Good, and you?" you take the opportunity to sniff. Why? What's the benefit?

Well, there are many. I'll start with the basic stuff. First, sniffing boosts your metabolism and your spirits. We humans are social creatures and we measurably improve our physical, mental, and emotional functioning when we connect with others. That's a medical fact. So there's an immediate, felt reward. Exchanging energy with another living being feels good—period. Dogs understand this instinctively. E-mailing doesn't do it. Texting doesn't do it. We need to mix it up with real people face-to-face. It keeps us alive, healthy, and vibrant.

Still skeptical? A recent study by Brigham Young University confirmed that social isolation is as bad for your health as smoking fifteen cigarettes a day, failing to exercise, or being an alcoholic, and twice as bad as being obese. People with healthy social interactions, on the other hand, have up to 50 percent higher survival rates (depending on their ages and the time frames studied).[17] Another study showed that elderly people who regularly engaged in simple social interactions—even if those activities did not involve physical exercise—lived two and a half years longer than those who kept themselves isolated.[18] Are we throwing away glorious health benefits

---

17 http://www.forbes.com/2010/08/24/health-relationships-longevity-forbes-woman-well-being -social-isolation.html

18 http://www.valueoptions.com/april06_newsletter/benefits_of_social_ interactions.htm

by avoiding one another like the plague? It would seem so. Candy Crush Saga and Farmville don't count, sorry.

Also, if you make a habit of sniffing, you create a sense of community around you—in your workplace, in your neighborhood, at the gym, at the supermarket. Since I began my personal experiment in sniffing, I can honestly say that the world around me has transformed. Everywhere I go, I feel "known." Some of the folks in my little universe know me well, others not as well, but it's a noticeably warmer and more intimate world I live in now than it was a few years ago.

Another great advantage to sniffing is that it makes a mark. When you stop and sniff, you leave an impression in the consciousness of another person. We always remember the people who listen to us and the people we listen to. As for me, I may be Hockey Guy to one person, Guitar Guy to another, Kayak Guy to another, Medicine Man to another, and Listening Guy to yet another. But however they know me, I am real and specific to the people in my world. So, if and when I need help with something, I have lots of people to turn to.

One of the most powerful rewards of sniffing is the almost magical way it leads to spontaneous opportunities. You never know when the person sitting next to you on a train or buying the cup of coffee in front of you may hold the key to your next business opportunity, your next job, or your entire life's direction. Unless you break your code of silence, you may never find out.

Sniffing leads to spontaneous opportunities.

You've probably had an experience that confirms this. You talk to a passenger on a train and it turns out the person works for the company you're trying to get into. You offer a listening ear to the mail carrier and it turns out she wants to buy the car you're selling. Over the years I have heard countless stories of people opening unforeseeable doors in their lives—meeting a future spouse, finding a new job, selling a screenplay, landing a multi-million-dollar contract, even one guy who ended up getting a personal audience with the Dalai Lama—as a result of "random" sniffing encounters. Often these encounters have an almost mystical component, as if Fate were somehow playing a role. In each case, though, the good fortune was unlocked only because the person *took the opportunity to sniff* or responded to a sniff from someone else.

Why Are We So Reluctant?

The benefits of sniffing are both immediate and long term. They can be mood-lifting, health-improving, and life-changing. Dogs make sniffing an integral part of their lives, like food, water, and oxygen. Then why don't *we* do it more often? Well, of course, some of it has to do with personality. Some people are introverts and others are extroverts. There's also the fact that technology, as we discussed, has made it so easy to avoid direct contact with one another. Thank goodness for the smartphone; we now have something to stare at besides the number display in an elevator! (I was waiting in line outside a popular take-out restaurant the other day and *every single person* in line was staring at a smartphone; no one was talking to the person next to them.) Aside from those things, it really comes down to fear. What is it we're afraid of?

By taking the risk of "being real" with another person, you become vulnerable on many levels. You run the risk of rejection, embarrassment, being judged, saying the wrong thing, looking like a crazy person who has no boundaries—or getting *involved* with a crazy person who has no boundaries.

You may well have a general discomfort level about self-revelation and intimacy, so you try, as a rule, to keep the social walls as high as you can. You know that when another person breaks that imaginary wall, anything can happen. The game changes. You're no longer in complete control (which is why the street hustler in Manhattan tries to make eye contact with you; he knows that once you've looked him in the eye, he can begin to work his magic on you). You prefer to stick to your little agenda—i.e., get from point A to point B as quickly and efficiently as possible—and avoid disruption.

That's the *real* fear, isn't it? Experiencing disruption.

Disruption

Disruption is rude and inconvenient. It throws off our neat schedules. It costs us time. It throws a monkey wrench into our plans.

But here's something to keep in mind. Disruption is not necessarily a bad thing. Disruption is inconvenient, yes, but it's also the engine of growth, opportunity, and adventure.

Every great leader and trailblazer in history has been disruptive. Jesus Christ was disruptive; Martin Luther King Jr. was disruptive;

Thomas Edison was disruptive; Gandhi was disruptive; Steve Jobs was disruptive.

Every great *invention* has been disruptive, too. The wheel, the printing press, the light bulb, the telephone, the computer. Each of these new ideas necessitated throwing out the old way of doing things, while messing up comfortable patterns and well-oiled systems. People lost jobs. Heads rolled. I'm sure the guy who owned Scribes 'R' Us was not too happy when Gutenberg came along.

Every important change in your personal life is a disruption, too. Falling in love, getting married, having kids, starting a business, moving. All of these things are major blows to your routines and comfort zones. But they often lead you to a better place.

Nothing changes without a disruption to the old pattern. Disruption ushers in the new, the creative, and the exciting. That's why entrepreneurs, artists, inventors, and innovators love disruption.

That's what's so refreshing about dogs, too. No matter what their agenda is at any given moment, they'll give it up in an instant if the opportunity presents itself to *engage* with another dog or a human being. They *embrace* disruption.

Whenever you stifle an instinct to go sniffing, it's an opportunity lost. How many times have you felt the urge to say something to someone, but you suppressed it and let fear take over? Then later you felt a twinge of regret or loss. That's the universe telling you, "You should have sniffed a little harder."

Stifling your sniffing instinct is an opportunity lost.

Start paying attention to that little gut feeling and acting on it more often. Take the risk of being a game changer.

The Art of Inviting

There is a difference, of course, between sniffing and being flat-out obnoxious. It can be a fine line, admittedly, but there *is* an art to sniffing without . . . er, cramming your face into someone's butt (my apologies to dogkind). You *can* sniff while practicing proper boundaries and being respectful.

We all know people who make us want to run the other way when we see them approaching. When *they* come sniffing, it feels pushy. Usually it's because they're only interested in *their* agenda, not yours. Their stabs at "intimacy" are thinly disguised attempts to fish for information that serves *them*, not you.

That's why we often recoil and clam up around salespeople. We know they're "sniffing" us out because they want to sell us something, and our natural reaction is to back off. Their energy feels pushy. Pushing energy almost always triggers a push-back or retreat response. It rarely leads to true engagement.

I like to use "pulling" energy instead. Pulling energy *invites* a response, without demanding it. If I run into someone with a dog, for example, I might make a comment that *can* be responded to, but doesn't *need* to be; e.g., "*Someone's* getting some sun today." If I run into someone at a conference who looks stressed out, I might reflect my observation back to the person, without layering on too much judgment. "Tough day? I'm all ears if you need it." If someone tells me he's "Good, good," but doesn't sound very convincing, I might say, "You don't sound too sure about that."

It's not so much the words you say—think of dogs; they don't use human words at all—but your tone and your intention. You make it clear that you are putting out an invitation to communicate but that you also understand that the other person may not be in the frame of mind to talk. You do both at the same time. You respect the other person's boundaries, while also tendering an offer to sniff.

Beyond the Casual Encounter

I've been focusing primarily on the "casual" encounters that often go untapped and unexplored. But, of course, "sniffing" is equally as important in your existing relationships—at home, at work, and in your circles of friends. You need to make efforts, on a daily basis, to dig beyond the superficial.

Women are naturally better at this than men. Men tend to "keep it casual," even when they're with close friends and family members. They'll stand around at parties, talking about sports and the hottest new app, while the women actually try to find out what's going on in each other's lives.

This story was recently brought home to me by my friend Jake. Every year, Jake and his old college friends get together for an evening at a designated restaurant/bar. They're all in their forties now, so this ritual has been going on for quite some time. Anyway, Jake was starting to grow weary of these get-togethers. Every year felt like a carbon copy of last year. They'd spend half the evening making small talk and then, after they'd had a few drinks, recite the same old stories of the "glory days." A few years ago, Jake decided to take a risk and try something different. He began the evening by asking each of the friends to talk about something difficult he'd been struggling with over the past year. Each guy was given "the floor" for as long as he wanted/needed, while the other guys just listened.

Jake said it was a remarkable evening. One of the friends shared that he had been struggling with unemployment for years but had been too embarrassed to talk about it. Another confessed that he was having serious health issues and had recently received an unpleasant diagnosis. None of the others had known this! Another told of a heart-wrenching problem he was having with his son. One of the guys expressed his desire to open up a store, but said he'd been too shy to discuss it for fear of being discouraged. One buddy would talk, the others would just listen. The shocking discovery, to all of them, was how little they really knew each other. By the end of the evening, though, there were tears and hugs and a whole new level of friendship. A new tradition was quickly established, whereby each of these annual get-togethers would begin in a similar way—each guy talking about a meaningful topic while the others just listened. This new ritual has transformed a casual "good-time" get-together into a real bonding experience, and some of the friends have begun spending more time together.

To me, this story illustrates how much value there is in sniffing. Had Jake not made the courageous decision to dig beneath the surface, these eight men might have remained superficial buddies forever, not true friends.

Listening Is a Gift

Humans have a fundamental craving to be *heard*—to be known, to be understood, to be received for who we really are. This is one of our most essential psychological needs. That is why listening is so important and why "sniffing" can be such a vital, life-changing practice. Whenever you give your ear to another person, even for a minute, and invite that person to share a bit of who he or she is with you, you offer them a tremendous gift. That gift makes an indelible mark on both the *listener* and the *one speaking*. Whenever listening takes place, a connection is made, just as when two dogs "check each other out" in their own inimitable way.

Humans have a fundamental craving to be heard.

So take it upon yourself to make your world a little more real. The next time you catch yourself saying, "What's up?" without stopping to hear the answer, or throwing out a high-pitched "Good, good," ask yourself whether there's anything you can do to make the encounter a little more genuine. It often takes only a few extra seconds. All you have to do is pause, set your own agenda aside for a moment, and truly *listen* to another human being. You will not only get an immediate, felt reward, you'll also be building a network that might very well provide your next sale, a great restaurant recommendation, or your next dinner date.

And that's worth sniffing for, wouldn't you agree?

Something to
Chew On . . .

Whenever I sniff out another dog, we come to understand each other better.

What if you made the effort—even just once a day—to "sniff someone out"? You can learn a lot about others.

It's fun to disrupt people. I do it all the time and they love it.

Benji

Benji, the loveable ragamuffin who is a film and TV star[19], was a pioneer in dog listening. The original Benji was rescued from the Burbank Animal Shelter by Joe Camp, the creator, writer, and producer of all the *Benji* films. Camp brought out the best in Benji for the world to see, and even created a method of dog training based on their work together. Essentially, the Benji Method works on two principles: compassion and communication. What Camp learned over the years is that dogs have amazing comprehension as well as a tremendous desire to serve and to please. To train a dog to do almost anything, you start with love and compassion. Then you communicate meaningfully with it. You don't bloviate. You communicate with purpose. A dog will literally do somersaults for you if you have a relationship based on mutual caring. "Nothing lifts the human spirit like sharing, caring, relating, and fulfilling," says Camp.[20] *Hmm*, feels like a lesson here.

Every Benji movie or video is unique because they're all told through the dog's heart and soul—there are no narrators or talking animals—just a floppy-eared mutt expressing emotions better than many human actors. As one critic put it: "Never before have I watched a dog's face on the screen as he considered problems, discarded alternatives, tested theories, decided on courses of action, executed them, then reacted to their successful or unsuccessful results." It's no wonder that Benji was the second animal ever to be inducted into the Animal Actors Hall of Fame.

---

19 There have actually been four Benjis over the years. While the next two Benjis were offspring of Benji I, the fourth Benji was also a shelter dog. This good deed not only gave us great movies, but helped the cause of animal adoption. According to the American Humane Association Benji's adoption and resultant screen popularity was directly responsible for the adoption of more than one million dogs.

20 *www.benji.com*

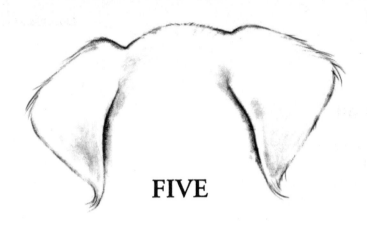

FIVE

Happiness Really *Is* a Warm Pup

*The only creatures that are evolved enough to
convey pure love are dogs and infants.*

—Johnny Depp

Your dog—or anyone's dog—can be a role model, if you pay attention. Think about it: when was the last time you heard one of the following statements?

- My dog is always texting while I'm trying to talk to him; it's so rude!
- Every time I try to talk, my dog keeps interrupting. He won't stop.
- I try to tell my story but my dog always has to "one up" me with her story that she thinks is so much better.
- Get this *dog* out of here! Please bring in someone who will really listen.
- My dog is such a phony; he gives you a big smile, but you can tell he's just trying to manipulate you. (Wait, that really may be true.)
- I can't even finish my sentence, my dog always finishes them for me—so annoying!
- My dog is so shallow; there's no basis for a relationship.

I have to tell you, I don't hear such comments very often. Probably the number-one thing we love about dogs is how genuine and caring they are. And how great they listen, well, when they want to, which fortunately is most of the time. Dogs seem *true* and *warm* in such an unforgettable way. No wonder they have so many friends! You need only to look in a dog's eyes to see their goodness and realness. There's a reason so many children's books have been written about dogs. Dogs are emotionally real. They have no pretenses. They don't play games. They express their feelings openly and honestly, rather than holding back or waiting to see how *you're* going to act. They don't have a hidden agenda. (And when they *do* have an agenda, there's nothing hidden about it.)

Dogs *care* about you, really and truly—to the point where they'll put their own lives at risk. There are countless stories of dogs running into burning buildings to rescue loved ones or allowing themselves to be harmed by an assailant in order to protect their people. Watch the way a dog worries over a sick or depressed family member. No one teaches them this stuff; they just do it.

The blog *The Science Dog* reports that "Dogs may . . . exhibit certain types of 'prosocial' behavior. These are spontaneous actions that are intended to help another individual in some way, usually with no obvious benefit to the helper. Psychologists have defined four general categories of prosocial behavior. These are comforting, sharing, informing, and helping. At least anecdotally, comforting is something that dogs seem to excel at."[21]

---

21 *http://thesciencedog.wordpress.com*

What do dogs get from you in return for all their genuineness and caring? Well, they get food, shelter, and warmth, sure. But they also get your undying love. The vast majority of humans have an overwhelmingly positive attitude toward dogs. We like, no *love*, them. In fact, most of us love them, perhaps more than any other species on Earth, including, in many cases, our own.

Here's a simple, but meaningful, exercise I lead when I'm conducting workshops or teaching a class:

Think of three people you consider to be really good listeners. These can be friends, coworkers, pets, famous people like Oprah or Dr. Drew, the UPS man . . . anyone at all.

Okay, give this some thought.

Take a minute.

Do you have three people? (Many do not.)

Take a look at your list.

QUESTION: Is there anyone on that list you don't like?

Point made.

So far, in all of the workshops I've conducted and classes I have taught, I've never heard a yes.

Why not?

We like people who listen.

They make a mark on us. We feel connected to them. We feel cared about. We feel heard.

We like people who listen. We feel connected to them.

NEXT I ASK THE GROUP: Who in this room considers him-self/herself a good listener? After the typical looking around to see how others are responding, most people in the room raise their hand. At this point I add, "So let me get this straight: (1) most of us want to be seen as good listeners, and/or (2) most of us think we *already are* good listeners." The latter point is the crux of the problem. We don't think we have anything to learn! When I ask workshop partic-ipants whether they have ever taken a course or read a book on listening—or, in fact, done anything whatsoever to consciously improve their listening skills—the response is overwhelming silence.

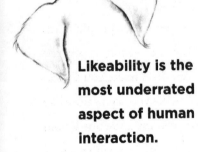

Likeability is the most underrated aspect of human interaction.

Likeability is perhaps the most important, but underrated, aspect of human interaction. The people you *like* are the people you hire, the people you do business with, and the people you seek out for relationships. In his book *The Likeability Factor*, Tim Sanders cites numerous studies that show:

- Likeability leads to career and leadership success;
- Doctors give more time to likeable patients;
- Likeable clients fare better in court;
- Likeable candidates are the ones who win elections;
- And likeable spouses have half the divorce rate of jerks.

So why not take a lesson from dogs, the most likeable beings on Earth? (Yes, yes, cat people, cats are likeable, too, but do they listen like dogs? Now that we settled that one, let's move on.) To be genuine and caring is one of the most powerful ways you can make a mark on the world—and make the world a better place while you're at it. Taking the time to listen to the people around you is the greatest and simplest way to do this.

Six Easy Steps to Genuineness

"Hold on," you might say. "What do genuineness and caring have to do with listening? If I want a lecture on how to be a better person, I'll watch a Wayne Dyer DVD."

Well, here's a key point. Are you someone whom people trust, like, and are drawn to? If not, then all the listening techniques in the world will not help you one bit. All they will do is make you appear slick and rehearsed, which, in the end, will make you seem more like a weasel than a dog. If, on the other hand, you *are* someone whom people like, trust, and are drawn to, then you don't need to worry so much about techniques and strategies. You'll do just fine without them. Just listen, with the goal of understanding in mind. Observing how a dog interacts with its loved ones reveals that the main thing that creates likeability is being genuine and caring—*truly* genuine and caring, not a seminar-learned imitation. Sorry, folks; you can't fake genuine.

You certainly have met salespeople, for example, whom you neither like nor trust. They smile and ask "personal" questions, and do "active listening" techniques that would put Dr. Phil to shame. You can't put a finger on why they give you the creeps, but by the end of an encounter with them you feel like you need a shower. These folks follow all the communication techniques they learned in their sales seminars—and do it very smoothly—but they operate from an unlikeable core, so you can't get away from them fast enough. In fact, you're repelled.

You've also probably met salespeople who share their humanness and vulnerability with you and seem genuinely interested in helping you solve your problems, even if their selling skills may be textbook awful. These people seem real and memorable to you. You like them, and, by extension, you usually like their products and services as well as the business that employs them.

What if, instead of getting caught up in the endless stream of selfish, output-driven communications, you made a real effort to be genuine with your fellow human beings and offer them a caring, concerned, and helping ear? What a way to make a mark in today's hurried, superficial, me-driven world!

What I'm talking about here can't be learned in a workshop called "Six Ways to Be Genuine and Caring." It has to be authentic. Dogs are a beautiful model for this. Dogs never use techniques and strategies on us (unless putting on the sad face to increase their treat count is one; then I stand corrected). All they know how to do is *exude* doggy goodness and authenticity. They can teach us all we need to know.

What It Means to Be Genuine and Caring

To be genuine means to:

- **Put people before techniques.** While it's a good idea to learn new interpersonal skills, it's also important not to put techniques before the person you are talking with. Salespeople are often guilty of this. Sometimes they're *working you*, and you can feel it. They use "intimacy techniques" like looking you in the eye and nodding, using your first name over and over like a mantra, and mirroring your body language. As a result, the whole encounter feels staged.

- **Be open, present, and spontaneous.** Genuineness is marked by a willingness to go with the flow. That doesn't mean you can't have an agenda, it just means you allow the conversation to find its natural direction and rhythm. Think of how your dog lives in the moment—your moment. You must be willing to give your agenda the backseat.

- **Have no hidden agendas.** If you do have an agenda for the conversation—and it's okay if you do—acknowledge it openly, in a way that feels comfortable for you. That might be through humor or a direct statement. *Hidden* agendas are what get you into trouble. When you have a hidden agenda, you're constantly manipulating the conversation to get your agenda onto the table, and the other person feels "played."

- **Be vulnerable.** Often you may be so concerned about looking like a pro or projecting your company's brand values that you turn up your professional shine at the expense of being human. You come across as slick or wooden. Allowing your vulnerability to show is one of the surest ways of creating a bond with the people you are talking to. It's okay to admit that you're feeling nervous or that you don't have all the answers. In fact, it's refreshing for others to hear and will likely result in a more positive encounter.

- **Allow feelings to show.** It's important to show emotion. That doesn't mean throwing chairs around the room in a rage, but it does mean letting your true feelings show to the extent appropriate to the situation. People who always show a blank face or hide behind a plastered grin are perceived as untrustworthy; you never know where they really stand.

- **Be yourself.** Being genuine also means letting your real personality shine. Very often, in professional situations, we adopt a corporate/"professional" personality at the expense of our own. When that entails behaving in ways that don't align with who we really are, we seem phony (because we are). Everything you do needs to be shaped by your real personality. If humor isn't your thing, don't start with a joke. To be yourself, the way a dog unabashedly is, is the heart of being genuine.

To be caring means to:

- **Be interested, not interesting.** You may secretly think you're the most interesting person in the room and may try to prove it every opportunity you get. It turns out, though, that interesting people are a dime a dozen. The really rare individual is the interest*ed* one; the one who passionately cares about what's going on in the lives of others. A caring person has the doglike trait of making others feel more important than him- or herself.

- **Be attentive to needs.** A caring person tries to understand what the other person needs or wants and listens for cues about this.

- **Have empathy.** To be caring means you notice the feelings of others and respond to them. For example, if there's just been a massive staff layoff, you don't crack jokes or try to be Mr. Motivational Speaker to the people heading out the door with their personal items in a box. Beyond just *noticing* feelings, the measure of a truly caring person is that you can *feel* others' feelings, at least to some degree. And you allow that to come through in your expressions.

- **Be kind.** A genuinely kind word or gesture can do more to create lasting bonds than all the "Winning through Power Plays" seminars in the world. A coworker once told me she was attending a weeklong workshop away from home. Every morning she passed a tollbooth and saw the same attendant there. One day he joked that her coffee looked good. So, on the last day of her seminar, she bought him a cup of coffee and handed it to him as she passed by. He instantly burst into tears of gratitude. Who knows what was going on inside this man? Is it possible he was in a very bad place and this one act of kindness made a huge difference in his life?

- **Be a giver, not a taker.** Finally, a caring person is a giver, not a taker. Though all relationships, business and otherwise, should be balanced—which means being able to take as well as give—caring people use no less than a 60/40 ratio. That is, they give at least 60 percent of the time and take 40 percent, and often give more than that. Be as generous as a dog with your time, your talent, and your resources, and it will eventually come back to you. (I wonder what the average dog's give/take ratio is? *Hmmmm.*)

Think about your interactions with dogs. If dogs make an impression, it's not because of anything they say—obviously. Rather, it's a quality of goodness they *exude*. By far the greatest way you can exhibit this quality is by opening up and listening to the people around you.

Think about it. If you've ever opened up to your dog when you were in a time of deep emotional pain—and I mean *really* opened up—think about how your dog acted toward you. I doubt that you will be counting the leash-law violations to describe its behaviors. The dog most likely simply stayed present and allowed you to express your feelings while exuding comfort for you. Be that same doglike comfort while being a quality listener. Let the other person vent. Let them cry. And if they don't have a dog—they're really going to need you.

Being genuine and caring is not a set of behavioral skills to be learned and demonstrated. It is not, in fact, any specific *thing you do*; it is an orientation you carry inside. A dog shows up with a wagging

tail because it's genuine, not learned
in a book called *How to Win Over
a Human in Two Seconds.*

**Being genuine
and caring is an
orientation you
carry inside.**

If you don't believe me, try an
experiment. Start your day with
the conscious decision, "Today I'm
going to have a caring attitude toward
everyone I meet and listen every chance I get." It's a lofty goal, but
see if you can make it until lunch. Before you enter each new setting,
refresh that attitude and remind yourself to give a few moments of
real listening to the people you encounter. Start with the people
who share your home then extend it out into the world—the coffee
barista, the security guard. If they share a remark with you, just pause
and take it in; absorb it with an attitude of truly understanding and
appreciating that person, if only for five seconds. When you get to
your office, do the same thing. Open up the space inside you to
caringly and unselfishly take others in. Here's my guarantee: if you
do this for an entire day, you will notice a profound difference in the
way you connect with people and the way people respond to you.

Do it for a week and you'll be canonized, or, better yet, "caninized,"
for sainthood.

But Aren't Humans Naturally Selfish?

After all, humans are naturally selfish, right? Asking us to set our
own needs aside is like telling a child to eat their vegetables: in
one ear and out the other.

Well, let's explore that for a moment. The argument over whether people can truly act unselfishly has been going on for millennia. Some say we're hardwired for selfishness; others are more generous in their view of human nature. But what I think everyone *can* agree on is this: it is usually better, for everyone concerned, if we *behave* unselfishly, at least in the short term. Because when we do this, not only do we meet the needs of the other people involved and help make the world a kinder, gentler place, but we also, more often than not, end up getting our own needs met. And in the long run, exceeded.

A marriage is a great example of this. When both partners make an effort, at least 60 percent of the time, to be unselfish in the small stuff, they not only make their partner happy, but they also get their own larger needs met over time. Why? Because their partner actually *likes* them and in return *wants* to do kind things for them. When both partners, however, are hung up on getting their own needs met in the short term, they turn off the other partner and create defensiveness and "counter"-selfishness. Neither party gets his or her needs met, and the world becomes a slightly stingier, nastier place.

The same principle applies in business relationships. Setting selfish needs aside in the short-term usually leads to greater benefits in the long run, *for both parties*, while also creating a more team-like, bonded, and positive atmosphere for everyone in the company. It's the ultimate win/win/win.

So, being genuine and caring turns out to be a smart business move. Dogs figured this out a long time ago. By putting their focus on *us*, they create such love and goodwill in us that we end up treating them as well as we treat the humans in our families, and oftentimes better. We generously offer them walks and toys and treats, given from the heart. We spend more money on our dogs than the GNPs of many nations. Because dogs are so faithfully and unselfishly devoted to us, we are triggered to be the same for them. We have

We have a trust that dogs are kindhearted and unselfish.

a trust that dogs are kindhearted and unselfish, so this allows us to be more unselfish toward them.

Give First, Get Later

What I'm suggesting is that you get into the habit of "give first, get later." We've heard this put in different terms, such as "Give and ye shall receive," or more currently, "Pay it forward." *Lead* with a caring approach. Serve the needs of the other party before worrying about how your needs are going to be served. Listen first, talk later.

Here's a recent example from my own career. I had a meeting set up with a high-level healthcare professional at a university medical center. We had only a

Listen first, talk later.

short time set aside for our meeting and I knew he was a very busy person contending with a lot of distractions. As soon as we sat down, I asked him (as I usually do) what was on his mind. It turned out he was hugely preoccupied with a problem he was trying to sort out. Recognizing that he needed to talk about his issue and that my agenda wasn't going to get his full attention, I flipped a mental switch and went into listen-only mode. I tucked away my agenda and decided to be a sounding board instead. Our time quickly burned up and he realized, apologetically, that he had spent most of the time talking about his issue and that we hadn't gotten to my agenda at all. I told him that this was no problem, that I was happy to listen, and that we could talk again at a later time.

Well, he e-mailed me within the week and scheduled a follow-up meeting. Perhaps because he was feeling guilty about talking my ear off, he wanted to give me some of his uninterrupted quality time. Long story short: I ended up getting this important professional's undivided attention for well over an hour. I got a fully attentive ear that I never would have gotten in the rushed and distracted half-hour that had been originally allotted to me. Was I unselfish to abandon my own agenda in our first meeting? Yes and no. It's true that I was willing to set my needs aside because I saw a person who needed a listening ear. So, yes, I *was* unselfish in the short term. But I also had faith that my "unselfishness" would pay dividends in the long run, and it did. As it almost always does. Unselfish? You be the judge.

I realize that to a salesperson, this idea seems to run completely against the grain of the ABC ("Always Be Closing") mentality. But by caring and giving, rather than trying to sell, you build goodwill and, dare I say it, good karma. If you make this generous-spirited approach a way of life—like a dog does—*you* will ultimately be the main beneficiary of your own generosity. But you may be wondering, *Why* does *it work this way?* Glad you asked . . .

The Benefits of Genuineness and Caring

Understand: I'm not talking about walking on water or multiplying loaves and fishes; I'm talking about being wise enough to delay your own gratification in recognition of the fact that good things come to everyone, especially you, when you give first. There are many selfish benefits to being "unselfish" in this way. For one, you activate the "rule of reciprocity."

What is the rule of reciprocity? Simply that people feel inclined to give to or do business with someone who has already given them something.

Make others feel genuine by offering an open, accepting ear.

Robert Cialdini, in his book *Influence: The Psychology of Persuasion*, cites several examples of the rule of reciprocity in action, including a lesson learned by the Hare Krishnas, a religious sect that used to raise money by dancing, singing, and asking for spare change in airports and on city streets. The result? People would cross the street to avoid them. Then the group switched tactics and began giving away flowers as *gifts* to passersby—no expectations stated. A different result this time. Their donations increased. People felt a responsibility to donate because they had been given a gift.

You can activate the rule of reciprocity by being the first person to listen. At the beginning of any meeting or encounter, both parties' minds are preoccupied with the need to get *their* agenda on the table. So why not use this to your advantage. Be the one who listens first.

Let the other party say whatever they want and need to say. This lowers their anxiety level and clears their mind; they are now more likely to be open to hear what *you* have to say.

You also create the "like" factor. By making yourself instantly likeable, it is more likely that people will want to work for you, hire you, buy from you, and hang out with you. You create "pull" rather than "push." Whenever you try to push an idea on someone else, there is an automatic "push back" response. On the other hand, when you show people that you care about them and are genuinely interested in what *they* have to say, you create a powerful "pulling" kind of energy. People are drawn to you and feel that they can open up.

Possibly the greatest benefit you gain from offering a caring, listening approach is that you learn a great deal about the other person and her particular situation and needs. By listening openly, you learn about the other person's personality and the things that are important to her. You learn about her needs and issues. You learn about her preferences and the things that turn her off. You learn about her values. You learn about the solutions that have been tried and failed. You are no longer working in an information vacuum. You are able to tailor your presentation, when the time arises, to a known set of needs and preferences.

Going to the Dogs—to Learn

There are probably a hundred psychological reasons why we feel relaxed and authentic around some people and guarded or misunderstood around others. But I believe one of the main ones comes down to the quality of listening we receive. The secret to making others feel genuine is to offer them an open, nonjudgmental, accepting ear. Again, think about the impact dogs have on us. If you've ever talked to one, you've probably felt freer and more accepted than you do when talking to most humans. That's because you didn't have to edit yourself or hold back or pretend to be something you weren't. The dog probably gave you pure, nonjudgmental, "receiving" energy. As a result, you not only felt the relief of being able to fully unburden yourself, you also felt authentic and at home in your own skin. Can we all please learn this simple lesson from dogs?

This need is clearly evident in romantic relationships. Over the years, as I've talked to others about what makes them comfortable in a relationship, one answer comes up more than any other: people love being in relationships in which they feel they can express themselves fully, with complete acceptance. That means having a partner who doesn't judge you or put up walls when you bring up certain topics. Rather, the partner listens to whatever you have to say and accepts it as your truth. Your partner doesn't try to censor you and doesn't get angry or hurt when you talk about topics that may seem weird or when you express an opinion on which the two of you differ. You feel completely free and *unjudged* around them. Unfortunately, this isn't how we're trained; most of us have been witnessing leash-law violations as our communication models since childhood.

Perhaps the most important thing to remember about being a caring listener is that it has to be done without selfish expectations. If you're thinking about your own rewards when you're offering a kind ear to someone else, you're actually being manipulative on some level. You're "steering" the conversation to your own advantage, and the other person—consciously or unconsciously—picks up on it.

This is the great paradox of selfishness. When you are always looking out for your own needs and trying to put your agenda on the table, you create push-back in other people. You lose, they lose, and the world loses. On the other hand, when you listen openly and genuinely, without any agenda—when you listen like a dog—you pull people toward you, rather than push them away. On a gut level, doesn't that seem like a better way to build long-term business and personal relationships?

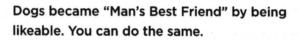

Something to
Chew On . . .

Dogs became "Man's Best Friend" by being likeable. You can do the same.

Focus on giving—not getting—most of the time. That's the only way I know how to play.

If you're genuine and caring, like me, you "pull" people to you. Then you don't have to push them.

Ricochet

Ricochet, a golden retriever from San Diego, has an extra-special talent—she's a trained SURFice dog®— and is the only dog on the planet who surfs with kids with special needs, those with disabilities, and wounded warriors and veterans with PTSD, as an assistive aid.

Ricochet has an ability to sense what people need, which in turn allows them to place their trust in her. This interaction fosters healing, empowerment, and transformation—opening up doors for them that were once firmly shut.

It all started in 2009 when Ricochet was going to surf with Patrick Ivison, a boy with spinal cord injuries, as a way to help him raise money. Before they got in the water, Judy, the dog's owner, said, "I could almost hear Ricochet thinking, *Patrick! Are you ready to surf?* . . . They were communicating like they'd been together a thousand times before, speaking to each other in a language that crossed species barriers and broke through incredulity." They were going to surf on the same wave but on their own separate boards. They rode a few waves like that, but then Ricochet jumped off her surfboard and onto Patrick's—and so her career of assistive, tandem surfing was born.

Since then, she's surfed with many adults and kids with disabilities. By listening to them with her heart, she adjusts her surfing style based on their disability, and gives them the confidence to try something they may have never imagined. Ricochet's gift and ability to communicate nonverbally has resulted in pure joy for many.[22]

---

22 For more about Ricochet's amazing power to heal, read her pawtobiography *Ricochet: Riding a Wave of Hope with the Dog Who Inspires Millions* by Judy Fridono.

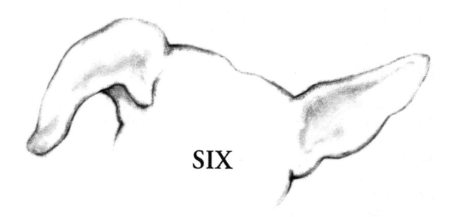

SIX

The Power of the Paws (Pause)

Bernie said nothing.
Silence is a tool.
He's told me that, and more than once.

—CHET (THE DOG),
FROM *THE SOUND AND THE FURRY*

Now we come to a disarmingly simple topic that always seems to generate more raised eyebrows than it should: silence.

Have you ever been with someone and neither of you is talking? After just a few seconds, you turn to the other person and ask, "What's wrong?" The answer is almost always, "Nothing." After a few more seconds of silence you ask the question yet again, only to get the same answer, but with perhaps a bit more annoyance. If you dare to ask one more time, you might have yourself an argument.

Why is silence such an uncomfortable and awkward topic, especially in the business world?

Remember the classic *Seinfeld* episode where Jerry and George pitch their idea for a pilot to a network executive? When asked what the show is about, George famously replies, "Nothing." Needless to say, their idea was a tough sell at first. After all, it's pretty hard to get excited about nothing. There's nothing to get excited about. Literally.

But it sold. And every episode of the actual *Seinfeld* series was about nothing, but yet about so much. And how did that work out?

Silence is a similar topic. Silence is the *nothing* of communication skills. It is simply the absence of output, right? Not exactly. Is it possible that silence has an energy that we in the West are only now just beginning to grasp? Is it possible that learning to harness the power of silence is a vital part of becoming a world-class communicator?

Dogs would say yes. Dogs are masters of silence and are completely comfortable with it. They have no need to compulsively fill the air with sound, like certain humanoids we all know. Sure, they bark, whine, or growl when they have a specific reason to, but then they quickly revert to their doggy-monastic state of silence. (Of course, there are dogs that bark all day long, due to living in the neurotic world of humans; but they are the noisy exception, not the rule.)

Because dogs don't speak in human language, they don't turn their world into a bunch of verbal symbols called words that they feel compelled to argue about, fret over, and fight for. Rather, they experience the world directly and accept it exactly as it is—which, come to think of it, is pretty much the definition of spiritual enlightenment.

One of the main reasons, I would argue, that we love hanging with dogs is that they *are* silent. Usually. (And when they're not, we take steps to remedy that.) One thing's for sure: there's no danger of dogs speaking to us in words. We know they're not going to judge, contradict, or advise us, so we feel relaxed in their presence. We feel able to be ourselves, to think our thoughts and express our emotions in complete safety. The only demands dogs put on us are frequent petting, and walks.

A Need for Silence

We humans, on the other hand, have an incessant drive to both emit sound and bathe ourselves in it. When we're not talking or making noise ourselves, we're listening to noise being made by some other human or by some electronic gadget programmed by humans.

Humans—at least humans in the modern West—are very nervous with silence. Perhaps that's because we don't have much practice with it. In our increasingly noisy world, it is almost impossible to get away from sound. Even in the refuge of our national parks, noise pollution—from planes, power boats, ATVs, car stereos, and other sources—is becoming a major issue. For most of us, when we do occasionally get a break from sound, the world feels blank. Empty. Missing something. And we feel a compulsive need to fill it in. The best example is leaving the television on during most waking hours while at home. Many of us get anxious when the TV isn't on because without it, we can't stand the silence. When we leave home, we leave the TV on for the dog because we know how much our fur babies can't stand the silence either. So we think.

But even as the world grows noisier and quietude becomes rarer, science is beginning to recognize the immense value of silence. Spiritual folks have always known this, of course. From Quakers to Buddhists to Roman Catholics, there is hardly a religious tradition on Earth that does not use "sacred silence" as part of its practice. But Western culture has been characteristically slow to catch on. Recently, though, scientists have begun to discover the inarguable

benefits of practices like silent meditation and some of the ways quietude aids in stress reduction, improved health, and more productive
thinking. Our noisy culture is finally being dragged, kicking and
screaming, into recognizing the need for silence.

One thing's for sure. If *you* want to become a doglike listener, you
will need to become a champion of silence. You'll need to recognize
and harness the power of the paws (pause).

I can honestly say that it wasn't until I began not only to tolerate
silence but *feel empowered* by it that I became worth a dime as a
communicator. I now see that silence is as integral to communication
as it is to music.

Silence integral to music? Well, sure. Think about what music
would sound like if there were no spaces between the notes, long or
short. It would have no melody, no rhythm, no form. It would be
just an ear-assaulting jumble of frequencies. In the same way, talk
without silence becomes just an onslaught of output, with no room
for creativity, understanding, or effective communication.

Awkward Silence

Ask a group of people to fill in the blank in the phrase, "[blank]
silence," and the majority of them will probably say, "awkward." Think about that. The first thing that comes to mind when
we think about silence is awkwardness. What does that say about us?

Of course, we don't *always* feel awkward about silence. Many of us
can enjoy staring silently at a sunset. Or lying silently in bed for a few
minutes. And one of the most comfortable types of silence, for many

of us, is the silence we experience in the company of dogs. We're *okay* with dog silence but not with human silence. Why is that? Maybe it's because we know that silence is natural and comfortable while with a dog. With humans, though, it's a different story. When people don't talk, it worries us. We feel uncomfortable. When someone enters a room and stands there without speaking, we shout "WHAT!" after about two seconds, because we can't stand the suspense.

Think about what would happen if you stopped talking for even one day. Within hours, family, friends, and coworkers would be in full panic mode. Psychiatrists would become involved—maybe even police.

That's because we *expect* each other to talk.

In fact, we almost *need* it. Humans actually derive psychological security from constant conversation. According to Dutch psychologist Namkje Koudenburg, "Conversational flow serves social needs . . . the need to belong, the need for self-esteem and the need for social validation." Silence, on the other hand, troubles us. According to Koudenburg's studies, it takes only four seconds of silence after a potentially controversial statement is uttered to make the uttering party feel "distressed, afraid, hurt, and rejected."[23]

When something we say is greeted by silence, we feel judged, alienated, and uncertain of ourselves. We know that others feel the same way, so we try to protect one another from distress. The result? Nonstop yammer. In fact, the typical measure of a successful social evening is that the conversation was constant and uninterrupted.

---

23 *http://www.nbcnews.com/health/four-seconds-all-it-takes-silence-get-awkward-1C6437340*

Silence is where true communion with another person happens.

But silence is where the good stuff is—much of it, anyway. Silence is the seat of creativity and wisdom. Silence is where true communion with another person happens. Silence is the birthplace of intelligent questions and innovative solutions. Silence fosters focus, clarity, and concentration; it provides critical rest and recovery for our brains. Silence is vital and essential.

So how we deal with the awkwardness issue is relevant.

Certainly, silence *can be* awkward. But if you want to be a powerful communicator, you need to develop a healthy relationship with that awkwardness. You need to learn not to feel threatened by it. That begins with learning to *sit* with silence, as a dog does; to just *be* with it—to *feel* the awkwardness, rather than try to fix it by saying something clever or by making noise. After only a little bit of practice in sitting with silence, a remarkable thing starts to happen. You not only realize that silence doesn't kill you, but you start to feel good with it. You start to get a taste of what I call "positive silence," as opposed to "negative silence." Positive silence is not a *lack* of something that needs to be filled; it is a powerful ground of energy. It is the place where composers go to write symphonies and scientists go to make "eureka" discoveries. The universe itself does its most brilliant work in silence—inventing a new flower, growing an embryo, coding DNA, spinning the planets . . .

If you want to become a good listener, it goes without saying that you need to learn to keep your mouth shut, to be physically silent.

But *dog* silence—positive silence—means more than just biting your tongue and waiting to commit your next leash-law violation. It means learning to work with silence as an actual tool.

He Who Speaks Loudest . . .

There is an unwritten rule in business and in social life that he who speaks the most wins. Whenever we out-argue, out-yell, and out-lecture others, we pat ourselves on the back. At a meeting, the person who holds the floor the longest, and makes the most noise, is often perceived as a leader of sorts. Unless the person comes across as an obvious idiot, he or she is accorded a certain level of importance. When we get the bulk of the airtime, we often have a false sense of victory. In fact, it is the very ability to control the flow of content that is often the mark of one's power status. Teachers hold a higher status than students. Speakers hold a higher status than audience members. If I'm more powerful than you, I can force you to listen to my rants, but I don't have to listen to yours. Silence, conversely, is seen as a sign of acquiescence.

The relationship between dogs and humans is a great illustration of this. We humans see ourselves as holding status over our dogs. Therefore, dogs are expected to bow (wow!) to our total dominance of the audio environment. *We* get to talk and make noise whenever *we* want, at whatever volume we choose. *We* get to decide whether there's going to be music or movies or video games playing. The dog is expected to quietly go along with our choices. But what happens when a dog won't stop barking? We put the dog outside. If the dog still doesn't stop, we yell, "Shut up!" That dog isn't coming back inside until he stops. The barking of a dog can drive us to the brink of insanity. We are annoyed by the sound itself, but even more, perhaps, by the violation of the power rule: Dogs are supposed to make noise only when we grant them permission (like, for instance, when we want them to "sing" on a YouTube video). Sound is power.

In his book *In Pursuit of Silence: Listening for Meaning in a World of Noise*, George Prochnik writes about a friend of his who experienced deafness for a period of his life and actually found the experience liberating. "Sound imposes a narrative," said the friend, "and it's always someone else's narrative"[24]—namely, that of the person who *makes* the sound.

This rule carries over to the workplace. In sales this is called "share of voice." Sales is far too often about getting more face time with the customer, which usually means time to deliver *your* message again and again. I am bewildered how we want to continuously increase our share of voice without necessarily understanding ("listening") to the customer first, and thus knowing what our voices should even be saying. Over the course of my career, I have gotten into disagreements more than once with colleagues and bosses who believed I should talk more often, and earlier, at business meetings and on teleconferences. This is a result of the output culture that most companies, and relationships, have adopted. My preference is to listen first and talk later; and to talk *if and only if* I have something of value to add. This habit has been seen, by some, as a hesitance to assert my status.

---

24 Prochnik, George. *In Pursuit of Silence: Listening for Meaning in a World of Noise*. New York: Doubleday, 2010.

I, of course, see it differently. By listening first—taking in the concerns, needs, and personalities of the parties involved—I can craft a more intelligent response. I feel I not only give respect to my colleagues, but also gain vital input that I wouldn't get if I yapped first just to strut my stuff. As a result, when it *is* my turn to talk, I believe what I have to say is more targeted and relevant.

Establishing dominance through talk, you see, is a short-term victory. Yes, you may win the alpha-dog peeing contest, but you don't necessarily win the hearts and minds of your listeners on a long-term basis. Your audience is forced to listen to you, but they are not required to buy anything you say. It's like the person on a date who talks all night about their life story and goes home feeling like the date went smoothly. Little did they know, the other party wanted to blow their brains out by the time they ordered appetizers.

Talking gives us a false sense of control. Though this kind of approach can produce one-off sales and short-term victories, it is not, I am convinced, an approach that leads to thriving collaborations and long-term relationships—in business or in your personal life.

Instead, I believe that silence gives you power in the long term. The key to making for-ever-lasting impressions is connection. And that means to be quiet and receptive. What if there was a way to measure how many times a salesperson listened to a customer instead of talking at them? Nah, this is not what comes naturally to

Share of ear: where we measure ourselves in terms of how much we listened.

us. Why not have a term, "share of ear," where we measure ourselves in terms of how much we listened? This approach will more often than not result in additional face time with that customer. "Share of ear" will allow people to talk about their favorite topic: themselves. How can you lose? We sure do have a lot to learn.

Let's explore some of the value we gain from using silence as a tool and why I am such a raving fan of it.

The Soundness of Silence

The benefits of silence could fill several books, but here are just a few.

Silence builds clarity and understanding. The human brain requires time and space to assimilate information. That does not happen when we assail it with data on a continual basis; the brain is so busy keeping up with the new input it can't process the old. Taking periodic pauses in the midst of a meeting or conversation allows the brain to catch up and "deal with information that was acquired during previous active states," says Andrei Medvedev of Georgetown University Medical Center.[25] After making sense of what it's been fed thus far, the brain can then ready itself for new input.

Silence allows us to focus. Processing sound waves is hard work for the brain. The more sound we hammer it with, the less processing power it has available for other tasks. Do you ever notice yourself turning down your car radio when you're lost or driving under

---

25 *http://www.foxnews.com/health/2012/10/18/when-youre-at-rest-your-brain-right-side-hums/*

stressful conditions? That's a natural instinct; you're buying more bandwidth for your brain to focus on what's important (in this case, *not* driving your Chevy Blazer into a signpost).

Silence aids creativity. Artists and writers have long sought silence as a way to aid the creative process. Note, for instance, that very few writers' retreats are held in bowling alleys or Zumba studios. Silent creativity is not just for solitary artists, though. Silence can lead to creative *group* ideas as well. Again, brain science may hold the key. According to an article in FoxNews.com's Health section, "Researchers found that during periods of wakeful rest, the right hemisphere of the brain chatters more to itself than the left hemisphere does. It also sends more messages to the left hemisphere than vice versa."[26] The significance of this is that the right side of the brain is the one most associated with creativity. And it feeds on silence and stillness.

Silence is good for our health. Though not directly related to communication, there is growing evidence that silence has enormous health benefits. "Noise, and especially noise over thirty decibels, is associated with high blood pressure, anxiety, and stress," says Dr. Paul Haider of *OmTimes* magazine.[27] Stress is known to lead to maladies such as depression, weight gain, heart disease, sleeplessness, high blood pressure, and a variety of ailments. Silence reduces stress. Formal practices of silence, such as meditation, have been scientifically shown to produce benefits such as stronger immune systems, reduced inflammation, lower blood pressure, faster healing,

---

26 Ibid.

27 *http://omtimes.com/2012/10/the-health-benefits-of-silence-simple-yet-profound/*

and increased fertility[28]—just from shutting up and letting the brain be quiet. This should serve as a wake-up call.

Coincidental note: dogs are good for our health and they reduce stress. The silent companionship of dogs is powerful. Far more than just irresistible cuteness.

Silence ignites appreciation. A busy, noisy brain is incapable of appreciation. This is perhaps why museums are typically quiet and why a "moment of silence" is universally observed to show honor and appreciation for someone who has passed away. Similarly, taking a silent moment to acknowledge a comment from a family member or team member allows you to digest and appreciate that comment before barreling ahead to the next topic.

Silence commands attention. As any good elementary school teacher knows, one of the most powerful ways to get attention is to go silent, rather than to yell and stomp your feet. When you lower your voice to a whisper or go completely silent, everyone turns in your direction. I routinely use this technique when talking to groups. I'll greet the room, and then stand in silence, waiting for everyone to stop talking and focus their attention to the front of the room, as they inevitably do. No need for me to be bossy or disagreeable. Just silent.

The explanation for this may again be rooted in our brain's functioning. According to an article in *The Telegraph* of London about a study on music and the brain, "The sound of silence stimulates a bigger response in the brain . . . *than music itself.*"[29] This is a truly

---

28 *http://foodmatters.tv/articles-1/7-health-benefits-of-meditation*
29 Roger Highfield, *http://www.telegraph.co.uk/science/science-news/3302414/Our-brains-crackle-to-the-sound-of-silence.html*

remarkable discovery. Science is starting to realize that the brain "hears" silence, not as an absence of noise, but as a distinct quality unto itself. (Spiritual masters have been telling us the same thing for 3,000 years, but hey, what do *they* know.)

Silence not only improves attention in the here and now, it also conditions the brain *to be better at paying attention in the future.* "Researchers at Harvard, Yale, and MIT," writes online author Bala Kanayson, "have found evidence that the practice of silence can alter the physical structure of our brains. Using brain scans they found significant growth in those parts of the brain that deal with attention and processing sensory input."[30]

Silence encourages participation and sharing. Just recently I was speaking with a large customer group with which I was unfamiliar. I kicked things off by asking the group if they had any topics they wanted me to address. There was some slight awkwardness as people looked around, feeling as if they should say something, but not having anything to say. So I said, "No problem. Why don't we take a few seconds of silence and see if anything comes up." By taking the pressure off them, I felt them breathe a collective sigh of relief, and then, within a few seconds, hands started shooting up. Ideas were flowing freely.

Nature hates a vacuum. By shutting your mouth and creating a vacuum of silence, you invite others to begin filling that vacuum with input of their own.

Silence indicates respect. By silently pausing after people say something, you indicate that their ideas are important. People feel they

---

30 *http://ezinearticles.com/?Silence-The-Mind-To-Stimulate-The-Brain&id=551258*

have been heard, as opposed to when you immediately jump in with, "Anyone else?" or "That gives me a great idea!"

Sold on silence yet? I hope so. So how do you begin to make conscious silence a part of your listening repertoire?

Zip It!

The first trick you'll need to learn is to zip it—your mouth, that is. I know that's a horrible thing to ask of you, but just give it a try. A stapler and duct tape may be required, at least for the first few weeks.

"Zip it" is my mantra. I tell it to workshop participants and to those I'm collaborating with. I tell it to colleagues and to friends trying to salvage wounded marriages. Most of all, I tell it to myself—all the time. I quietly whisper, "Zip it," in my mind whenever I feel the urge to talk coming on like an itch while knowing I have nothing vital to contribute.

"Zipping it" is not easy. The urge to talk is a deeply ingrained habit that comes very close to being a compulsion. But you would greatly benefit by learning to control this compulsive habit. Fortunately, the rewards are enormous and you can begin to experience them right away.

As I said earlier, it's amazing how programmed we are to talk and how little training any of us has had on the art of staying silent, especially in business. Salespeople, managers, teachers, business presenters—we all focus almost exclusively on how to deliver output. Yet the *input* of others is where the true treasures lie. That's where we learn about others' needs and desires, the unique challenges they are facing, and the world they live in. That's where we form real connections.

If we want to sell people on what we have to offer (and we are all salespeople, in one way or another), we are much better off listening to our "customers" first—whether those are lit-eral customers or team/family members we

The input of others is where the true treasures lie.

need to sell on our ideas. That means, as a general rule, spending much more time in "input" mode than "output" mode: a.k.a., "zipping it."

Of course, I don't mean you should *literally* remain silent through-out business encounters. It would be pretty distressing for all con-cerned if you were to stroll into a client's office and just sit down and stare at him or her. What I do mean is that in each encounter you should zip it as soon as comfortably possible.

If you are visiting a potential client, for example, you might want to introduce yourself and explain a little bit about who you are and why you are there, but then flip the focus back onto the client at the earliest opportunity. Ask some open-ended questions. Ask about *his* situation, *her* concerns, *his* unique needs. Then zip it! And *keep* it zipped, perhaps as much as 80 percent of the time. You'll then be able to tailor your eventual pitch to what you have learned from the client. It has often been said that people will sell *themselves* on your product or service if you let them talk. So let them.

Even professions as content-heavy as teaching and training can benefit from zipping it. Think about the most dynamic and effective teachers you've ever had. Were they the type who marched up to the podium and read from a dog-eared (sorry) set of lecture notes for fifty-five minutes? Or were they the type who sat with the students in a circle, engaged them, asked stimulating questions, and spent a lot of time listening to what the students had to say? I recently spoke to a former college professor who told me that the day he became good at his job was the day he threw away his lecture notes. He started delivering *much* less pre-programmed content and spending more time finding out what the students wanted to learn from him, and then responding to that. Needless to say, his teacher evaluations went from mediocre to superb, as did the students' learning.

Zipping it is equally effective on the personal front. Think about the people you love to call on the phone versus the ones you prefer to avoid. The latter are probably people who routinely talk your ear off, right? Okay, now think about yourself. Which list do you fall on for others—their "avoid" list or their "call now" list? Scary thought, isn't it.

It's funny—and kind of sad—when you realize how much effort we expend to keep our *dogs* quiet. We're embarrassed and frazzled when they break their silence, even for thirty seconds when the UPS truck shows up. Some of us go so far as to use a muzzle, or (ouch!) a shock collar to keep dogs quiet. But we never notice how much "barking" *we* do. If we put one-tenth the effort into silencing ourselves that we put into silencing our dogs, we'd be veritable Zen masters.

Harnessing the Power
of the Paws (Pause)

When you're in speaking (versus listening) mode, you can build silence into your communications by embracing the "power of the paws." Simply pausing and not saying anything at all is an extremely effective communication technique.

Watch a great actor on film, or better yet, on stage. The most gripping parts of the performance are often when not a word is being spoken. Every good actor knows that the pause creatively involves the audience. When the actors are speaking, you see, the audience is busy processing what's being said; they are in a passive, receptive role. But during pauses, the audience members are drawn in as participants. They sit forward in their seats. They become co-creators of the drama, filling in the spaces with their own ideas. Pausing literally pulls people forward. A pause also:

- **Grabs attention.** Pauses keep the brain of the listener active and dynamic. We expect non-stop talking, so we are often caught off guard by a pause.

- **Creates suspense and mystery.** When a pause occurs, the audience/listener wonders what's coming next.

- **Signals importance.** Pausing after a statement implies that the speaker wants the listener to really absorb what was just said.

- **Gives the listener time to think.** Periodic silences give the brains of listeners time to digest, process, and "connect the dots."

- **Gives the speaker time to collect his/her thoughts and summon intuition.** By deliberately pausing at frequent intervals, speakers buy themselves time to think about what they're going to say next and how to say it most effectively. They are also able to tap into their intuition.

Periodic silences give listeners time to digest and process.

- **Creates a comfortable rhythm.** Just as silence between the notes is a vital aspect of music, periodic silences in speech give it a more appealing and dynamic rhythm.

I consciously use the "power of the paws" *all the time*. If I'm starting a talk and I don't have everyone's attention, I'll pause and say, "Let me know a good time to start talking," and then I'll pause again. If I'm meeting with a busy physician and he's giving me only partial attention while he fills in charts, I'll just pause. Within seconds I'll have his full attention. Some of my friends have noted my use of the pause while on the phone, and have come to appreciate my effort to not commit leash-law violations. Whenever I'm speaking to a group, I'll pause periodically, look around the room, and make eye contact with audience members. Kill them with silence!

Silence Is a Gift

As I've noted already, a major reason we feel so free talking to dogs is that we can count on them not to say anything. We sense that they're "with us" as listeners but we know they're not going to offer advice or criticism. Dogs give us the gift of silence. And silence truly is a gift. It's one that we can give each other, too. With a little practice. Okay, a *lot* of practice.

When someone wants to talk to us, we often make the mistake of thinking they're seeking our input. Occasionally that might be true. If your neighbor's computer has suddenly crashed and you are a techie, for example, your input might be highly desirable. Most of the time, though, people are just looking for a listening ear. *They* want to talk. They want *you* to listen. They do not necessarily want you to share, advise, criticize, judge, or volley for serve.

Human beings, it turns out, have a remarkable ability to solve their own problems, given the time and space to do so. Remember that scene in *Wedding Crashers* where Vince Vaughn is pouring out his soul to the elderly priest at the breakfast table? Vaughn's character rambles on about his romantic tribulations, while the priest just sits there nodding and smiling. At the end of the scene, Vince arrives with tremendous insight. He thanks the priest, calls him an "enlightened cat," kisses him on the mouth, then walks away, happy and content. Of course, the joke is that the priest hasn't said anything at all. But Vince somehow feels he has been counseled.

That's a large part of how therapists work. Their main role, contrary to popular opinion, is to not offer advice or "cures." They are trained to direct clients to *discover* insights. Their main role is to get the client to open up about important personal issues and to encourage him to keep talking. Eventually, with enough guided expression, the client (at least in theory) discovers truths for himself that illuminate the steps that need to be taken. Like the customer who talks herself into buying a product, the therapy client often talks herself into healthier life choices, with the skillful guidance of the therapist. Dogs perform a similar service for us when they let us talk things out with them. Roamy did that for me.

When we offer the gift of silence, we offer people the gift of discovering their own solutions. And the solutions people arrive at themselves tend to stick, whereas solutions crammed down their throats by well-meaning friends tend to be discarded like junk mail—unsolicited and undesired.

The gift of silence is a sacred thing. My friend Susan is a hospice volunteer. Once or twice a week she goes and sits with a dying patient. One of the first things hospice workers are taught is to be silent and to ask questions rather than tell stories, give advice, or talk about themselves. Their role is to offer the gift of silence so that the dying person can talk, if able to do so, about whatever is on *his* or *her* mind. Or say nothing at all. What a wonderful service. It's fascinating, though, that we offer it only to dying people. Think about that. A person literally has to be on his deathbed to earn the right to a silent listener!

Oh, by the way, guess who the most popular volunteer is at the hospice program; a dog named Charlie. Just saying . . .

The gift of silence shouldn't only be for people who are dying or struggling with life crises. Try it in your dating life, for example. Meet someone for coffee and spend most of your time just listening in silence. Let the other person talk about his or her life, asking a question now and then to show your ongoing interest. Odds are, you'll be pursued with interest after this. You might even hear comments like, "I just felt really connected to you," or, "For some reason, I feel you *get* me." If you want to give your romantic life a major bump, you don't need looks, money, charm, or devastating coolness—just an ability to quietly listen.

A New Culture of Silence

One thing you'll need to get used to if you decide to embrace silence in your life: some people are going to think you are marginally nuts. Don't worry, you'll get used to it; I did. Though we love our dogs for remaining silent, we don't know quite what to make of it when our fellow humans do the same.

People around me have grown accustomed to my pauses, if not entirely comfortable with them. I have been using the "power of the paws" long enough that people now respect my methods and have even grown curious about them.

One thing I find helpful is to *explain* my silences as I use them. For example, when I start a talk, I may say, "Let's take a silent moment to think about what you'd like to learn." If I'm making a business visit, I might tell my host, "I'm here to listen and gather information, so I don't plan to talk too much." When I'm in a conversation, I'll say, "I want to sit for a moment with what you just said," before going silent for a couple of seconds. In other words, I *frame* my silences so that others don't feel anxious about them and so they understand what I'm up to. My pause lets them know that I am listening, and thus they feel heard. After a while, people begin to accept this as my style, even if it's still foreign to them.

Here's a telling question to ask yourself if you're a dog owner. Did your dog bark today? Odds are, you'll remember if it did. "Sure, he barked for twenty seconds when the meter man showed up." Why do you remember the dog barking? Because it was set against many hours of silence. Did you ever see any of the Kevin Smith movies featuring Silent Bob? Bob, true to his name, doesn't say much. But when he does, it's usually taken as profound. I still remember his insightful speech in *Chasing Amy*. This is a common technique in Hollywood: create a character who hardly ever speaks, so that when he or she *does* talk, the audience sits up and pays attention. It's a simple fact: what you say is taken more seriously when it's not part of a constant stream of noise. The less you talk, the more weight your words often have.

Something to
Chew On . . .

I'm a master of silence. Take a lesson from me.

Go for the "power of the paws." Saying nothing is a great way to get attention.

Hey humans, try zipping it. Don't always do that nervous talking thing you love to do.

Rin Tin Tin

When you hear the name Rin Tin Tin, you probably think of the television series that ran in the 1950s, and you might suppose he was one of the earliest dog stars. But, the fact is, there were movies featuring Rin Tin Tin as far back as 1922. Lee Duncan, who rescued the dog as a pup from a bombed kennel in Germany during World War I, directed Rin Tin Tin with voice commands, as he had an excellent ear for cues on what to do next. He secured his first acting job when Duncan ran across a Hollywood film crew having trouble getting a wolf to do what they needed for a shot. Duncan proclaimed that his dog could do it in one take. When the dog lived up to the promise, both Rin Tin Tin and his owner were hired on the spot for *The Man from Hell's River*, launching a new silent film star and literally saving Warner Brothers as a film studio. When funds were running low, they'd truck out another Rin Tin Tin movie.

Duncan honored his dog in a poem, describing him as "Alert and ready for my slightest word." But the really amazing thing is that Rin Tin Tin often proved to be a better actor than his silent film human counterparts. Many silent actors, limited by not being able to speak, over-acted—emoted, in a manner that often seems a little silly when seen today. As Susan Orlean points out in her book, *Rin Tin Tin: The Life and the Legend*, this special dog acted far more naturally than the human, since he wasn't dependent on speech. So he became a perfect silent hero. He starred in over twenty films, always getting top billing over established human actors, and had his own live radio show. He was even nominated for an Oscar, though something of a scandal was created when the Academy of Motion Picture Arts and Sciences changed the rules prior to the ceremony to say that non-humans couldn't win an award.

When Rin Tin Tin passed away in 1932 at the age of fourteen, most radio shows were interrupted to broadcast the news, and every major newspaper worldwide carried the story, with many also posting an obituary. Some headlines described the death as a tragedy and an insurmountable loss! However, his legacy lives on, as well as his family. The Rin Tin Tin bloodline of dogs are trained as service dogs to provide assistance to special needs children.

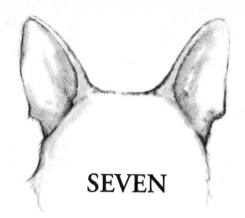

SEVEN

Heel, Sit, and Stay: The Art of Patient Attention

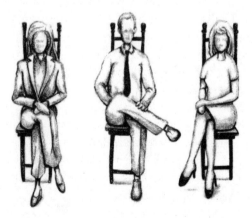

They [dogs] never talk about themselves
but listen to you while you talk about yourself,
and keep up an appearance of being
interested in the conversation.

—Jerome K. Jerome

One of the most extraordinary talents of our beloved four-leggeds often goes unnoticed. Perhaps that's because it lacks the wow factor of other dog tricks, like catching Frisbees in midair, running like the wind, or tracking down a criminal from one whiff of his sock drawer. But it's no less awesome. I'm talking about the ability of dogs to stay put and do *nothing but pay attention.* Once a dog is trained to heel, sit, and stay, it is able to withdraw its attention from the world of distractions and place it fully on its "master," watching intently for the next cue. The dog won't do this for just a few seconds until it is captivated by the next shiny object that comes along—like a human would—but for *as long as it takes.*

A trained dog's attention is a marvel to behold. Have you ever watched canine obedience trials, for example? Between commands, the dog will remain perfectly still, its eyes riveted on its master's eyes and hands with a focus that's almost tangible, like a power cord connecting the dog to its owner.

A dog that has not been trained will run off after the first squirrel that grabs its attention. But a dog trained to heel will stay glued to its human partner, never getting a step ahead of him, ignoring the hundreds of sights, scents, and sounds that are trying to pull its attention in every direction. The trained dog knows its *job* is to follow its human's lead, and it dedicates itself to this job with a single-minded seriousness of purpose. It makes its human the center of its world, shutting out any and all distractions.

We humans admire this type of discipline in our dogs and even give out prizes for it. But most of us don't hold ourselves to the same standards, especially when it comes to listening. We don't realize that listening is a job that requires 100 percent of our focus. We are forever getting ahead of the person speaking, and running off after the first verbal and mental squirrels that catch our attention. Most of us, to put it bluntly, have the attention span of an untrained puppy.

But imagine if we could train ourselves to see listening as our *job* and devote ourselves to mastering it with the same motivation a dog has.

Heel, Human, Heel

We humans desperately need to learn the art of heeling. By heeling, I mean to:

- Mentally slow down and stay *with* the person speaking, not run ahead of him;
- Make the person speaking the absolute center of your attention;
- Shut out mental distractions;
- Resist the impulse to interrupt and take the lead in the conversation.

Good luck with those, by the way. Heeling is very difficult for most humans. We have restless, itchy minds. We are easily triggered by distractions—both internal and external.

One of the reasons we have trouble "heeling" as listeners is that our brains can think much faster than our mouths can talk. Humans can speak about 125 words or so per minute, while our brains can think at about 400 to 500 words per minute.[31] This means that whenever you're processing a fellow human's 125-word-per-minute verbal output, your brain has a lot of bandwidth available to do other stuff. And that's exactly what it does. Not only does it think about what kind of salsa you're going to buy to go with tonight's fish tacos and how nicely the speaker's lipstick matches her scarf, but it also thinks of clever ways you can top the speaker, speed up the speaker, or work your own agenda onto the table.

The trick to being a great listener is to focus your brain's "spare" processing power on things like: trying to better understand what the speaker is saying; making full use of your eyes, ears, and heart; and signaling your attention to the speaker. To do all *these* things

---

31 *http://edis.ifas.ufl.edu/he748; and http://www.au.af.mil/au/awc/awcgate/kline-listen/b10ch5.htm*

well actually requires the *full* power of your brain. You just need to consciously harness that power.

The human mind is like an untrained dog. To get it under control requires training. Dogs allow themselves to be trained to heel because it earns them Liv-a-Snaps; you need to recognize that you, too, earn rewards through heeling.

The Payoff

What's to be gained by training yourself to heel and pay focused attention? Well, we've already identified the many long-term benefits of better listening—such as building lasting relationships, becoming a more likeable person, and triggering the rule of reciprocity—but here I'd like to focus on a few *immediate* rewards you gain:

You create a bond with the person talking. The surest way to create an instant connection with another person is to give the person your undivided attention. It's almost like magic. Attention from another person is *felt energy.* Earlier I talked about some ways our eyes and hearts beam measurable energy to others. Though this may sound New-Agey to some, it is consistent with quantum physics. Did you know, for example, that a photon of light behaves differently if a human is watching it? There have also been experiments that

You create a bond with the person talking.

have shown the power of focused attention to affect the growth of plants,[32] the shape of water crystals,[33] and the behavior of random number generators.[34]

You don't need a physics lab to prove it to yourself, though. Try this simple experiment: the next time you are in a group or audience, give your undivided, laser-like attention to the person on stage. This can be a teacher, a public speaker, an actor, or even a musician or dancer. Just beam your attention at that person. What you may discover is that the performer begins to single you out and direct his or her performance (speech, lecture, etc.) at you. This isn't your imagination. Attention is like a magnet. When you give someone attention, you form a connection like that between a dog and its trainer.

You make the speaker feel honored and respected. Few things, if any, are more inherently rewarding to a human being than to be given attention. Receiving attention makes us feel validated, confident, and worthy—as if our ideas, and our *selves*, have value. Countless times in my career, I have been invited to follow-up meetings or out to lunch—I have even launched business relationships—as a direct result of being the one person in the room who paid silent attention. Attention is noticed. It's appreciated.

You acquire the content. Another huge benefit from heeling— staying *with* the person speaking—is that you not only *hear* the information being shared, but you *acquire* it. There's a big difference between hearing and acquiring. When you only *hear* something, it

---

32 *http://www.spindriftresearch.org/examples.php*

33 *http://www.masaru-emoto.net/english/hado.html*

34 The PEAR (Princeton Engineering Anomalies Research) lab experiments have been described in numerous books, such as Dean Radin's *Entangled Minds* and *The Conscious Universe.*

passes in and out of your short-term memory. When you *acquire* something, it goes into your long-term mental toolbox.

A gentleman I know went through college on a full scholarship and graduated magna cum laude, and yet he rarely took notes or studied. Many of his peers assumed he was an off-the-charts genius, but he explained it in much more mundane terms. "I hate studying, so I put all of my attention on *getting* what's being said. That way it becomes part of me and I don't need to study it." Almost without exception, his teachers assumed he was the brightest student in the class, simply because he was so tuned in. They would often read an extra layer of wisdom into his test answers and give him the highest grades in the class, even if he didn't have the facts perfectly memorized. Something positive almost always comes of heeling. There are a couple of habits you can develop that help greatly with this.

Stop and Acknowledge

If there was one piece of advice I could give you to quadruple your effectiveness as a listener overnight, it would be this: stop and acknowledge. That is, after a person makes a comment, pause and acknowledge that you've heard it. This one step—stop and acknowledge—could probably cut the national divorce rate in half. The main reason conflicts escalate is that one or both parties do not feel heard and acknowledged by the other. Party A, not

Acknowledgment is a *fundamental* communication skill.

feeling heard, ratchets up the intensity of the rhetoric, which, in turn, makes Party B more defensive. Party B then amps up the rhetoric, and the whole debate just escalates, because no one is hearing anyone else. Leash-law violations are occurring at an alarming rate. True connection has not taken place and resentment rears its ugly head.

Acknowledgment is a *critical step in communication*. The idea is so powerful and yet so simple: after someone speaks, acknowledge what has been said *before* defending yourself, coming up with a better idea, jumping to the next topic, or asking for a third party's input. What could be simpler? Acknowledgment allows people to feel respected and valued, creates an atmosphere of two-way communication, and defuses tensions before they have a chance to mount.

And yet acknowledgment is a step that is almost universally skipped in politics, business, and personal relationships. We jump straight into reaction mode.

Why do we miss this essential heeling (healing) step? Part of the problem, I think, is that our culture teaches an adversarial, I win-you lose form of communication. We're trained to think of every conversation as a debate that we need to *win*.

Turn on any television talk show and what do you see and hear? Talking heads trying to get the last and loudest word. Even in a format as innocuous as sports talk radio, all you hear are hardened opinions vying to score points. I do a lot of driving, and in all of the radio talk shows I've ever listened to over the years, I have rarely, if ever, heard one party stop, take in what the other party was saying, and respond, "Wow, I never thought of it that way; I'll have to rethink my opinion. Thanks for helping me see things differently."

In fact, as audience members, we hate it when people do that. We see it as wishy-washy. When a politician changes her stance on an issue, we view it as flip-flopping, instead of as evidence that she is capable of listening to other points of view.

Again, acknowledgment is a step that is almost universally skipped in politics, business, and personal relationships. Perhaps it is because *we actually see listening as a weakness*. After a political debate, we praise the candidate who spoke the most firmly and loudly and who commanded the microphone the longest, not the one who showed indications of listening. Culturally, we admire

Acknowledgment is a step that is almost universally skipped.

strong opinions that remain undimmed by facts, better ideas, or the input of others. On Facebook and other social media sites, it is common to see solo rants masquerading as conversations. Strange, isn't it?

Conflict is entertaining. No one wants to watch a TV show in which everyone listens to and acknowledges each other—*boring!* We want to see drama. If sparks don't fly, we change the channel.

A fascinating example of this is the *Dr. Drew* show. When it first aired, it was one of the few models of good listening on TV. Dr. Drew would sit one-on-one with guests and really try to hear things from their point of view. Dr. Drew is in fact a very good listener—I have had the pleasure of meeting him in person. But his show's format was later changed to one in which Drew is shown on a divided screen with four or five guests, all vying to out-talk one another.

Makes for better TV, evidently.

Here's the issue: what's entertaining on a talk show or effective in a courtroom is not necessarily what's productive in business and relationships. And yet we use this adversarial model in all situations. It works something like this:

1. Form a strong, unchangeable position.

2. Enter a "conversation" with the intention of proving yourself right and the other party either wrong or ignorant.

3. Do not listen to or acknowledge the other person, except to find springboards for your next point.

4. Use every tactic available to out-talk the other party until your opinion achieves victory.

It's not surprising then that in so many meetings, conversations, and encounters no one feels heard. "Hearing," after all, is not the goal; winning is.

Imagine if a dog tried to out-bark you every time you gave it a command. How long would you put up with that? But a dog doesn't do that. It acknowledges your words and patiently awaits your cue as to what to do next. Even if the dog is bursting with eagerness to play a game or go for a ride, it will eventually force itself to put its own agenda on hold and wait for you. If a "lowly" beast can exercise this kind of self-control, can't we humans learn to do the same? Yeah I get it; humans are the master and dogs are . . . *blah, blah, blah*.

Ever wonder why man isn't man's best friend, but dog is?

Toward a Better Model

For many of us, the concept of acknowledging another person's point of view is so foreign that we need special training. Consider a couples therapist in action. A big part of the job is to teach couples to stop and acknowledge what the other party is saying/feeling before stating their own point of view. Often this is like pulling teeth. The parties are so busy *reacting* that they literally have no idea what the other party is feeling or saying. Sadly, they often don't care. They are there for their own agenda.

How do you know when the speaker has been acknowledged? When the speaker *feels* acknowledged—*not* when you say he or she should. In many professions, one of the most common complaints from customers and clients is that the service professional—doctor, lawyer, car mechanic, salesperson, hair stylist—didn't really listen to them and acknowledge their concerns and wishes.

The speaker's acknowledged when the speaker *feels* acknowledged.

What I find fascinating is that in professions where clear communications can be a matter of life or death, there *is* some form of acknowledgment built into the communications protocols. Take, for example, this model for communications between a pilot and an air traffic controller, posted on the SKYbrary website (*www.skybrary. aero*):

Starting with the "Transmit" step, the ATC (Air Traffic Controller) transmits an instruction to the pilot. The pilot *listens*, then *acknowledges* receipt of the message by carefully repeating back what he heard from the ATC. The ATC then *listens* and confirms or corrects what the pilot said. Finally, the ATC *acknowledges* the whole communication as understood, and the loop is closed by granting clearance for landing. These steps are completed every single time, as part of protocol. Imagine if they weren't!

Other emergency responders such as fire, police, military, and rescue teams have similar communication protocols. They include acknowledgment as a vital part of the communication process. That's because communication cannot be said to have occurred unless both parties have acknowledged that the communication has been heard and understood.

Strange, isn't it, that we recognize the importance of acknowledgment when lives are at stake, but we disregard it the rest of the time? Lives may not literally be at stake in most conversations, but the quality of your relationships, both business and personal, certainly is. It is definitely safe to say that we often downplay the importance of what is being said by failing to acknowledge it. We also invalidate the other person, leaving them feeling unheard, and perhaps sending other negative messages we're unaware of. One major consequence of lack of acknowledgement is that you trigger resentment. You may walk away from the exchange not realizing this has occurred, but the other party has made a mental record of it.

What if, instead of using the adversarial model for conversations and meetings, we employed a model that demonstrates constraint while acknowledging your speaker.

The Heel, Sit & Stay Model (HSS)

1. **Listen to the other party without interrupting.**
   And here's a twist: actually consider what is being said.
2. **Pause.**
3. **Acknowledge what the party has said** and demonstrate an understanding of the other party's position (or ask to clarify if necessary).
4. **Weigh the new input against your tentative position.**
   Adjust your position if needed.
5. **Communicate your position** (revised, if appropriate) to the other party.
6. **Return to Step 1**, rinse, and repeat until the communication loop is complete and you are cleared for landing.

I urge you to read through these steps a couple of times in order to appreciate their importance and to let them become a part of you. They most likely appear foreign so repetition and practice may be in order. Acknowledgement may not necessarily be a "one time" event in a conversation, however. Sometimes multiple points are made, each worthy of acknowledgement. Other times the speaker may not feel acknowledged, so your repeat performance may be in order. Yeah, yeah, I know, once was enough . . . so you think. Don't worry, you'll get through it—and thank me later.

Let's Stay Here for a Moment
(Stay, Staaaay, Staaaaaaay—Good!)

Acknowledgment is not only important in one-on-one communications, it's also vital in group settings. Again, it's amazing how often this step is skipped. Very often, in groups, things like the following happen:

- A member of the group will offer a comment or give an answer to a question. The meeting leader will then immediately say, "Next," and move on to another participant.
- A group member will be trying to make a point and the leader will allow another member to interrupt and spin the conversation in a new direction.
- The leader will use a group member's comment strictly as a springboard to get to *his* next idea.
- The leader will ignore or minimize a group member's comment because it's not the answer she was fishing for.

These habits, and many more like them, are the norm in groups. That's why, when I'm conducting a meeting, a class, or a workshop, I often stop and say, "Wait; let's stay here for a moment." By this I mean, "Let's stop and take in *this* idea before moving on to the next one." Not, "live in the moment," which is a great quote with tons of merit. Staying here means to accept and absorb what was said. (Yes?) I try to do this whenever a group member provides input or an idea (or person) is getting glossed over too quickly.

It often seems to me that 80 to 90 percent of the valuable ideas contributed in meetings are lost or forgotten because we just use them as transitions to the next idea. We nibble on an idea for a second, and then toss it aside like a drumstick with most of the meat still on the bone (something a dog would never do!). "Let's stay here for a moment" tells the audience to heel, to slow down, to pull some tasty meat from *this* bone before charging ahead to the next one. Impatience is something many of us suffer from nowadays, partly because technology has trained us to want everything now, now, now. As a society, we are losing our ability to focus on any one thing for more than a few seconds, let alone minutes.

What would happen if we could learn how to sit back, take a deep breath, and give our full attention to one another? Sometimes it's not your turn to drive the car, but just to be the passenger. And when that's the case, do what a dog would do—stick your head out the window, feel the breeze, and enjoy the ride.

Drastically Lower Your Interruption Rate

Another step you can take toward becoming a better heeler is to consciously reduce your interruption rate. This pays big-time dividends. As you know, interrupting is a major leash-law violation, and can more accurately be described as an epidemic in our society.

We humans have a nearly physical urge to interrupt one another. Dogs don't. Oh sure, they interrupt us now and then, but only when they have a pressing need—to go outside, to tell us something is wrong, to inform us that (horror of horrors) the mailman is coming. We humans interrupt because we have an inner psychological itch to do so. We need to become aware of this itch and learn how not to scratch it.

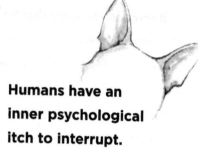

Humans have an inner psychological itch to interrupt.

Where does the itch to interrupt come from? I think the immediate cause is often a feeling of anxiety. When we're listening to someone talk, we begin to feel anxious that we're not going to get "our turn" to speak. So, we begin strategizing about how we're going to insert a crowbar into the conversation. The longer the other party speaks, the greater our anxiety grows until the itch to interrupt becomes unbearable and our mouths spring into action.

A big key to getting this habit under control is to become *aware* of the anxiety before acting upon it. Very often, the simple step of noticing an anxiety is enough to manage it. It seems to be the nature of anxiety to build and build until it erupts into a compulsive action. But often if you simply *notice, acknowledge,* and *feel* an anxiety, it loses its intensity, and the compulsive behavior (e.g., interrupting) is averted.

By becoming conscious of your anxiety, you can work on lowering your interruptions-per-minute rate (IPM).

Gauging Your IPM Rate

What's *your* IPM rate? You probably don't know. But I guarantee that if you make an effort to become aware of it, it will begin to decrease just as a result of that awareness.

If we were able to measure the factors contributing to our IPM rate we could probably create a quasi-scientific formula (accent on the "quasi"). The variables, as I see them, are: 1) our *reason* for interrupting (R); 2) our available *ways* to interrupt (W); 3) the *mitigating factors* for or against our interrupting (MF); and 4) our *anxiety level* (A). So our formula for calculating IPM might look something like this (no need to take notes, class):

$$\frac{(R + W + MF)2}{A} = IPM$$

Silly? Yes, a bit. Practically useful? Not really. But before we disregard it *completely*, "Let's stay here for a moment." Perhaps by becoming just a *little* more aware of the factors that affect our decision to interrupt versus keeping our mouths shut, we can gain a little more mastery over our IPM.

Okay, so let's look at these factors a little more closely.

Reasons for Interrupting (R)

The urge to interrupt can be like a physical itch that we scratch without even knowing why. Simply asking yourself the question, "Why am I interrupting?" can be a giant step toward getting your IPM under control. There *are* some good reasons for interrupting, which we'll soon talk about, but there are also a lot of reflexive, thoughtless reasons that may not be so great. Here are some common ones:

- Boredom, or the feeling that "I've been listening long enough"
- Discomfort with the subject matter
- The urge to grab the steering wheel of the conversation
- The desire to show off your knowledge, wisdom, experience, etc.
- Disagreement with something the speaker said
- The feeling that the speaker needs *your* help to express himself better
- The urge to finish the speaker's thought to show you're on the same page

You can probably think of many more. Rule of thumb: a good reason for interrupting is one that serves the *speaker*, the group, or the conversation itself (e.g., "You're going to miss your flight if you don't wrap up"). A bad reason for interrupting is one that serves only you, your ego, or your neurotic need to make noise (e.g., "My aunt in Duluth had an even funnier experience . . .").

Ways of Interrupting (W)

Just as there are many reasons for interrupting, there are many *ways* of interrupting. Some of these are meant to cut the other party off instantly; others are meant to cause the speaker to interrupt himself/herself. Examples of both include:

- Jumping in and talking over the other person
- Raising a finger and opening your mouth

- Coughing pointedly
- Frowning or making expressions of disapproval
- Sighing or yawning
- Cutting off eye contact, looking away
- Looking at a clock, watch, or cell phone
- Gathering your belongings
- Texting someone

And, of course, in today's tech-heavy world, there are also numerous ways we interrupt one another in chat rooms and text conversations, such as sending emoticons, changing the subject, or abruptly logging off. ("Listening" is just as important in a text conversation—though much easier to fake!) It's a good idea to become self-aware regarding your own interrupting behaviors.

Mitigating Factors (MF)

There are also many mitigating factors that make us more or less likely to interrupt others. These often operate in our subconscious. By becoming more conscious about these factors, you can make better decisions about whether to let them influence your behavior.

- **How well you know the other person**—we tend to feel more comfortable interrupting someone we know well (but should we?)
- **The state of your relationship with the other person**—for example, the more strain there is in the relationship, the more quickly you'll tend to interrupt

- **Your passion/expertise about the topic**—it is hard to refrain from interrupting when it's a topic you *love* to yap about
- **Time constraints**—if you have only a few minutes and the speaker is rambling
- **Hierarchical roles**—the greater a person's status, power, and/or celebrity, the less likely you are to interrupt

Of course, you're not going to memorize my IPM formula (nor should you)— it's complicated, which illustrates how much "stuff" we bring to the table with our communication. However, the more awareness you have about your own interruption tendencies, the easier it will be to refrain from scratching the interruption itch.

Training Rules

I once watched a dog trainer working with another person's dog, using hand signals. At one point the dog just started barking, nonstop. The trainer became annoyed, but from my point of view it was clear: the dog just didn't understand the signals it was receiving. Perhaps the dog's own trainer does the signal differently. The dog didn't know what to do so it just started barking.

This is what often happens in conversations. Sometimes we just don't understand the conversational signals

The problem is that conversational signals and rules are not universal.

and rules. The problem is that the rules are not universal; each of us has a different understanding of them and respect for them, and each culture has its own rules and expectations.

Consequently, we often don't know who should be grabbing the conversational lead and running with it. The result? Chaos. Just turn on a topical talk show if you want to see what I mean.

It would be handy if we taught our kids universal rules for listening, but we don't. (We expect them to be expert listeners even though we model poor listening to them!) That's why structures like parliamentary procedure and Robert's Rules of Order get invented. I'm not suggesting you should adopt formal and rigid rules like those, but it does help to have *some* mechanisms in place to handle interruptions and speaking privileges.

If you're running a meeting, for example, it might be a good idea to appoint a moderator. It becomes the job of the moderator—and *only* the moderator—to keep the meeting running in a smooth, focused, and timely manner, and to make sure everyone has a turn to speak, and allowing participants to be heard. The moderator, and only the moderator, has interruption privileges. If someone needs to weigh in, he or she can raise a hand but may speak only when recognized by the moderator. Though this might seem restrictive, it frees up the rest of the group to listen fully and attentively without worrying that someone is going to commandeer the conversation.

It's also a good idea to have your own personal set of guidelines that you follow in conversation. These can help you manage *yourself* and make sure you spend plenty of time heeling. A few of my own guidelines, for example, are:

1. If it's my role to start the conversation, I will briefly introduce myself and the issue at hand. I will then give the floor to the other person immediately, asking for his/her point of view.

2. I will not interrupt the other person unless there is a major misunderstanding (e.g., the person thinks I'm there to sell him a second-hand cemetery plot).

3. When the other person finishes speaking for the first time, I will pause, acknowledge what he/she said, and offer some kind of positive feedback, even if I disagree with the substance of what was said (e.g., "I'm glad you feel you can be honest and direct; that's what I was hoping for").

I have many other "rules" I try to follow. These are not to restrict me or to inhibit spontaneity, but just to help ensure that I spend as much time as possible heeling and don't go running off into the woods, chasing squirrels and dragging others behind me on a leash.

Unlike dogs, no one is going to train you to heel; you need to train yourself. With a little thoughtful training, you will be rewarded with more positive encounters, the Liv-a-Snaps of listening.

Something to
Chew On . . .

You need some training in order to listen better. I'll go get the leash.

I love to be acknowledged. So does everyone else.

For Dog's sake, try not to interrupt so much.

Lassie

Everyone knows Lassie, either through images, movies, or TV reruns. Lassie was a gorgeous collie who never wasted her "words." When she whined or scratched at a door or barked out of a window, you knew she had something important to say. Everyone dropped what they were doing to listen to her. Often Timmy, her human companion, was almost comically sensitive to her communications—"What's that, girl, you say the barn's on fire and the piglets are trapped? Let's go!" But the point is, people listened to Lassie. Why? Perhaps because she was silent most of the time, so when she did "speak," she had everyone's attention. It was usually a life-or-death situation. She certainly never cried wolf. It's no wonder that Lassie was the first animal ever to be inducted into the Animal Actors Hall of Fame.

As is often the case, the most entertaining fictional accounts are based on amazing real events. According to British writer Nigel Clarke in the *Shipwreck Guide to Dorset and South Devon*, the real Lassie that inspired so many films and television episodes saved the life of a sailor during World War I. Half-collie Lassie was owned by the landlord of the Pilot Boat, a pub in the port of Lyme Regis. On January 1, 1915, the British battleship HMS Formidable was off the coast of South Devon when it took a hit from a German submarine's torpedo, tragically losing more than 500 men. Winds from a storm that came through following the incident blew a life raft containing bodies along the coast to Lyme Regis. The Pilot Boat pub offered its cellar as a mortuary.

Lassie found her way downstairs and began to lick the face of one of the victims, Able Seaman John Cowan. She stayed beside him for more than half an hour, nuzzling him and keeping him warm with her fur. To everyone's astonishment, Cowan was alive and eventually stirred. He was taken to the hospital and went on to make a full recovery. If not for Lassie, her astute powers of perception and quiet insistence, Cowan surely would have been one of the victims of this tragedy.

EIGHT

Beyond the Bows and Wows

*Dogs are better than
human beings because they
know but do not tell.*

—Emily Dickinson

If you have spent any time with canines, you know they have an uncanny ability to understand your intentions and feelings, even though they don't understand most of your words. Or perhaps it's *because* they don't understand most of your words.

While dogs do recognize certain key words that are important to them—hence the perennial need of dog owners to *spell* the word W-A-L-K when making casual reference to a certain perambulating activity—science does not believe that dogs have the ability to process the finer intricacies of language.

Yet dogs seem to have little difficulty understanding what's on your mind, especially if it involves *them*. A recent study indicates that dogs process emotional information in voices in much the same way that humans do.[35] Surely you don't know any dogs that have trouble figuring out when their human is thinking:

---

35 *http://news.sciencemag.org/brain-behavior/2014/02/how-dogs-know-what-youre-feeling*

- Let's play
- Snack time
- I'm angry at you
- I love you
- Maybe I'll take the dog for a walk
- I could use a couch companion right now
- I'm worried today
- It's bedtime
- I'm not feeling well
- Time to pack the suitcase for my trip
- Time to go pee
- I think you're the cutest thing ever

Some of a dog's mindreading talent seems to boil down to a "tele-pathic" ability of some kind that we still don't understand. There is plenty of accumulated evidence to suggest that dogs (as well as cats and other animals, in some cases) have the ability to foretell a disaster, such as an earthquake, tsunami, or air raid; know when their humans are on the way home, even from another state or country; and find their way home from impossible distances. A friend of mine, Andy, has told me that his dog—a papillon—always knows when he, the "master," is *thinking* about taking the dog for a walk, even when the dog is not in the same room with him. Andy has done experiments with this. He just sits at his desk and does nothing but think the thought, *Maybe I'll take Milo for a walk.* Within a few seconds Milo comes trotting in from another room and starts jumping up and down. Good luck to Andy if he changes his mind now. Wait, who did we say the "master" was?

But whether you believe dogs are psychic or not, you must acknowledge that they are uncannily sensitive about reading our moods and intentions.

The Power (and Weakness) of Words

What makes dogs so good at reading us? Some of it boils down to their coevolution with humans. Their well-being has long depended on being able to figure *us* out and they've done a masterful job of it. But, of course, they've had a major handicap as well: they naturally don't understand *our* language. (At least we don't *think* they do; maybe they chat about economic policy when we're not listening.) As a result, they've learned to pay incredibly close attention to our nonverbal cues, which is where true human moods, feelings, and intentions are broadcast.

We humans, on the other hand, are hooked on words, so we often fail to give the nonverbal stuff its due. Our ability to use language makes us lazy. Words have definite meanings, so it's easy to just accept them at face value: to literally "take others at their word." The problem is that such a small part of our communication is expressed by words, as mentioned earlier. The rest is conveyed by facial expressions, body language, tone of voice, and other clues such as context of the remarks and the personality of the speaker. That means if you take people only at their literal word for things, you'll not always get an accurate response. I'm not suggesting that if your friend tells you the movie starts at 7:30 not to believe him, but I am suggesting that if your significant other says that she is "just fine" while her arms are crossed, you may want to investigate further . . . by listening.

What Lies Beyond the Words

Here are some of the crucial aspects of communication that are typically left out of the words.

Feelings. Human beings are emotional creatures. In fact we *live* in our emotions. How we *feel* is the critical element in just about every aspect of human life. Put two people in the exact same house, with the same income, and the same set of life circumstances; one may feel happy and fulfilled, another may feel trapped and isolated. Same exact set of facts but a very different reality. Why? Different feelings. Human life is *about* feelings. And feelings are subjective.

To know how someone will behave, you need to know how he or she feels.

I tend to believe that feelings are primary, even in matters like politics and religion and philosophical/scientific beliefs. You *feel* your way through life and then you come up with intellectual opinions to justify your feelings. What that means for listening is this: if you want to know how someone is going to behave, you need to know how he or she feels. This is as true in business relationships as it is in personal, intimate relationships.

Dogs know this. They tune in to your moods and feelings and use them as a guide as to how they can best "play" with you.

The problem with text-only communications is that the feeling element is either missing completely or widely open to misinterpretation. The reader fills in the feeling *he or she* believes was present in the writer's mind, which, in my experience, is wrong far more often than right. If a friend sends a text with just a few short words (for example, "We need to talk"), you might read terseness or crisis into the note when, in fact, she may just have been in a hurry or in a meeting. What *she's* feeling is, "I miss you and can't wait to talk to you"; what *you're* feeling is, "Uh-oh, she's ticked!"

True intentions and meanings. Words are crude tools for conveying a speaker's intentions and meanings. To illustrate this, a common exercise in acting classes is to go around the room and have each actor say the same simple line, like "Hey, come here," with a different intention, such as threat, seduction, conspiracy, or friendship. It soon becomes obvious that the words themselves are just a fraction of the complete intention being communicated. The difference is tone. When given a choice between believing the words and believing the tone, we almost always, and wisely, side with the tone.

Dogs go right for the good stuff. (Try telling a dog "Everything's fine" when you're feeling miserable, and see whether or not it buys your words.) You must learn to do the same. Whenever you're listening, you need to have one antenna up for what the real intention of the communication is, beyond the language. We humans are shockingly inept at this; we give words too much credit.

Honesty/sincerity level. On a related note—and this may come as a shock to you—human beings often say one thing while meaning another. How many times have you told someone (or has someone told you), "I'll call you soon and we'll get together," or, "I'm going to give your suggestion some thought," or, "Let's just be friends," while having absolutely no intention of following through?

When reading text messages it is difficult to determine someone's sincerity level. On the phone, it is a bit easier, but still can be tricky because you can't see the person's face (especially the eyes) and body language. In person, you have a much better shot at getting it right— provided you watch the nonverbal language.

Comfort level. When talking with someone live, it often becomes obvious—*if* you're paying attention—when a person is feeling discomfort about the subject matter. Everyone has his or her own unique way of signaling discomfort, but a few common ways are: breaking off eye contact; tensing up physically; aiming the feet or body away; or rubbing the face, neck, or other body parts. According to energy psychologists, people instinctively rub certain acupressure points on their bodies to give themselves comfort. So, when you observe someone doing this, it's a pretty good indication that something is making them *un*comfortable.

Hidden issues. Very often, the topic being discussed is a stand-in for a deeper, broader issue. When your spouse starts screaming irrationally about the way you stacked the dishes in the dishwasher, odds are that something more than dishes may be at stake here. If you choose to believe dishes are the true issue, dishes may soon be flying in your general direction.

Both in business and in personal life, people feel more comfortable talking about small, concrete, specific issues rather than about larger, deeper, and more painful ones. As a listener, you are not getting the true meaning of a communication if you miss the larger issues behind it.

Needs. One of the prime things to listen for is the need being expressed by the speaker. After all, if someone is taking the time to talk to you, it's generally because he or she needs *something*; you should probably learn what that is. So, two main questions in your mind should be: (1) "What does this person need from me ultimately?" and (2) "What does this person need from me *right now*?" In other words, what role does this person need you to play in this conversation. Should you simply be listening and providing a sounding board, or should you be offering help? Should you be brainstorming with the person or only listening to *his* ideas? Should you be shutting your mouth and taking instruction? Should you be cheering this person up? Challenging him? Helping him clarify his thoughts?

Dogs are constantly trying to read your needs and play a role that's helpful to you. If you're grief stricken, the dog seems to know you need comforting and is going to snuggle with you. If you're just feeling sorry for yourself, the dog might do something goofy and funny, as if to say, "Get over yourself and play with me."

Subtext

In literature, there is a concept known as *subtext*. You probably remember it from American Lit 101 or Intro to Drama. Subtext is just what the word suggests—it is a level of meaning *below* the written text, or below the spoken words. In drama, the subtext usually carries the real meaning of a scene.

A fine example of subtext from a modern-day movie is the scene in *Sideways* where Paul Giamatti's and Virginia Madsen's characters have a long conversation about wine, but what they're *really* doing is feeling each other out about a possible romantic encounter. As they discuss the way wine reaches a peak and must be consumed at precisely the right time, you can feel the romantic possibilities for the evening reaching *their* peak and then souring like old wine as the Giamatti character fails to "make his move" at the right moment. Anyone who thinks that scene is really about wine might actually be drunk.

Subtext is not just a literary thing; it exists in real life, too. A big part of listening like a dog is learning to pay attention to it. What is the person really saying? Often people speak symbolically or indirectly about things they are not comfortable discussing in plain language. An argument between a husband and wife about dirty socks left on the floor might really be about, "I don't feel supported and appreciated in this relationship." A discussion about a damaged phone line at the office might really be about the disconnect between executives and middle management. Because dogs don't understand most human words, they deal with subtext most of the time.

It's possible to pick up subtext in e-mails, text messages, and in phone conversations as well—sometimes it's intentional, sometimes not—but it's easier to detect when you're talking to someone live and in person. There are simply more clues to observe.

In drama, it is said that writers provide the text and actors provide the subtext. It's the actor's job to show the levels of meaning and intention that are not conveyed by the words alone. How does the actor do that?

One powerful way is to speak and behave in a way that is out of sync with the words being spoken. The actor conveys, by his tone of voice, his facial expressions, and/or his actions, that there is more to what he is thinking or feeling than the words alone are conveying. An example might be a scene in which you see a husband sweetly telling his wife over the phone that he loves her, but meanwhile he's staring at his watch, rushing to a restaurant for a date he's planned with another woman on an out-of-town business trip. You know he is contemplating infidelity. You don't need to have it explained; all you need to do is witness the incongruity between his words and his physical behavior.

Congruity

Congruity is a great concept to keep in mind as a listener. When people are fully on board with what they're saying, there is congruity between their words, tone, their energy level, their facial expressions, and their body language. For example, if they're introducing a cool new business idea and they're truly excited about it, their voices will be excited and higher-pitched, and their gestures will crackle with energy. When people mean what they say, their faces and bodies express the same emotion as their words. Dogs are almost always fully congruous. That's why we trust them so much. You rarely see a dog playing ball with its head hanging despondently. Only humans do that kind of thing.

Whenever you see *in*congruity, you know there's more going on than the words are saying. Dogs are very good at spotting incongruity,

and they let you know they're concerned about it. If you say, "You're
a good boy" to them in a harsh, angry tone, or, "Do you want to go
for a walk?" in a sleepy tone while crawling into bed, the dog will
cock its head and look at you as if an alien embryo had just burst
from your chest. Even subtle incongruities make a dog nervous.
Something isn't stacking up in the dog's mind; the words don't match
the tone of voice or the body language, and the dog knows it. So it
doesn't quite know how to process what you're saying.

When there *is* full congruity between what you say and the *way* you
say it, both dogs and humans accept that communication at face value.

Humans, as a rule, are not very good liars. That's why great actors
make the big bucks. Most of us have trouble "selling" a position we
don't really believe in. Our face and body don't get completely on
board, so there is usually a "tell" of some kind. The human body has
a natural inclination to be honest, even if the conscious mind tries to
lie. So when you are forced by circumstance (or by your own devious
mind) to say something you don't fully believe in—and this probably
happens a dozen times a day—part of you feels compelled to send
out the message, "I don't *really* think this." You unconsciously use
incongruity to do this.

You also *deliberately* use incongruity at times. A classic example
of this is the spouse who goes around loudly slamming household
objects. When asked what's wrong, she invariably replies, "Nothing."
Of course, what's being announced with every fiber of their being is
that something *is* wrong. The incongruity is so obvious it might as
well be wearing a clown costume.

If this person's mate were to take the word "nothing" at face value and reply in a chipper tone, "Great! Glad to hear it; I was just checking," a human volcano would likely erupt. What is expected in this situation is for the mate to try to tease out the real truth—or else get used to sleeping on the couch.

Humans are generally reluctant to express strong ideas and emotions that might cause conflict, embarrassment, or hurt feelings. So we do not, as a rule, go around expressing these feelings directly. We prefer someone to *pry* them out of us than to express them openly and directly. We use incongruous behavior as a way of saying, "There's more to this than my words are saying."

As a listener, then, you need to be attuned to incongruity, even in subtle forms. You don't need to study NLP (Neuro-Linguistic Programming) or become a body language expert; you really just need to step back, observe the speaker, and ask yourself whether the words, the facial expression, the tone of voice, and the body language are all sending the same message. If not, what's the deal?

Listeners need to be attuned to incongruity, even in subtle forms.

Signs to Watch and Listen For

When looking for signs of incongruity, some of the things you might want to notice in the speaker are:

Energy level. As a general rule, the more strongly a person is feeling an emotion—positive or negative—the higher his/her energy level will be. Have you ever been at a business meeting when the speaker puts his hands in his pockets, looks down at his feet, and dully drones something like, "I'm tremendously excited about our new market-ing initiatives." Really? Lack of energy signals lack of belief, lack of commitment, lack of the claimed emotion.

Of course, some people are naturally demonstrative and others are not. Not everyone jumps up and down when they love an idea, but they usually signal their energy level in *some* way: a gleam in the eye, an excited hush in the voice.

Tone of voice. If the speaker's tone of voice is not matching the message his words are carrying, that is usually significant. It tells you the emotion is not real. It's hard to fake an emotion vocally. Part of the reason is physiological. When you're really feeling an emotion, it changes your vocal instrument. A tense jaw muscle gives a different shape to your mouth than a relaxed one and creates a different sound (which dogs and other sensitive listeners pick up on). A smiling mouth sounds different from a neutral one; a smile can be heard over the telephone and gives the voice a distinctive quality. Painful emotions, on the other hand, tend to constrict the throat and pro-duce a "choked-up" sound, which again are very hard to fake. If you watch a good voice actor at work in a recording studio, you'll notice that she acts her lines out with her face and often her whole body, even though no one's going to *see* her performance. That's because she knows that unless she is physically experiencing the emotion, it won't come across in her vocal instrument.

Facial expression. People do all sorts of facial gymnastics as they speak. Typically, they *try* to project an emotion appropriate for the situation. But they often fail miserably, flashing glimpses of more honest emotions. If you want to know what someone's *really* feeling, look into his or her eyes. The eyes have a hard time lying. A smile that doesn't come from the eyes signals insincerity. Similarly, looking away or to the side or breaking off eye contact are often signals that honesty has fled the scene like a thief in the night.

Many people are simply unaware of their own facial expressions and broadcast their emotions pretty baldly. All you have to do is observe them critically. Clenched teeth while saying, "Congratulations," or probing, suspicious eyes while saying, "I trust you" are telling signs.

Dogs read our faces like the open books they are. That's why they often seem to "psychically" know what we're thinking before we say a word.

Posture/body language. Most people are surprisingly unconscious about their body language, too. I could fill a book with examples of how body language communicates hidden meanings; in fact, many such books *have* been written. A lot of the "expertise" in this area, however, tends to be pretty dogmatic (sorry, dogs, for that word)—e.g., touching the face means lying, standing over someone means dominance, etc. I believe body language is more complicated and individualized than that. Personality, upbringing, ethnicity, and many other factors come into play. Folded arms may mean one thing for you, another for me. Still, there are some obvious and fairly universal signs you can watch for.

When a person says, "I'm open to your opinion," but is blocking her body with an object, perhaps there is more to the story. When a politician says, "Yes, absolutely!" but is shaking his head *no* (I've seen this numerous times, and my jaw always drops), you might want to question his sincerity.

With a dog, of course, what you see is what you get. There's never a disconnect between its thoughts and its body language. If it's hungry, it will paw at its food bowl; if it wants to be close to you, it will throw itself onto your lap.

When it comes to reading human body language, I suggest relying more on observation and intuition than an encyclopedia of meanings. Simply ask yourself, *Are his posture and gestures in line with the spoken message?* Your gut will usually give you a reliable answer.

Speed/timing. Another thing to be aware of is timing. If a person is slow or hesitant to respond, it may be an indication that she is not fully on board with what she is saying. Part of her is holding back. You won't pick this up in a text or e-mail, obviously, or even necessarily in a phone call, but you will see it in a live person (yet another reason for meeting face-to-face when possible).

On the other hand, if the person seems to be rushing or speaking too fast, it could signal nervousness, lying, or a desire to "pull a fast one" on you. It's similar to when the offense rushes to the line of scrimmage in a football game, hoping to get the next play off before the opposing coach throws the challenge flag.

What's not said. One of the most meaningful aspects of a conversation is the part that isn't said. Again, most people have a natural aversion to lying, so they try to avoid directly saying things they don't believe. Often they do this by saying nothing at all.

If three people at a meeting are gushing about a new product and a fourth person is saying nothing, odds are that person has reservations.

When you strongly feel or believe something, you naturally want to put that feeling into words. You want to go on record. So when you do *not* do that, it usually means something. A classic example from the realm of relationships is when one person says, "I love you," and the other replies, "Thank you."

When interpreting nonverbal communications, take in the *whole* of the communication. Turn yourself into a biological antenna, the way a dog does, and *feel* for a sense of congruity. Is everything adding up? Do the words I'm hearing go together with the expressions and behaviors I'm seeing, the gut feeling I'm getting, and the tone of voice I'm hearing?

Again, the eyes and the heart are as important as the ears. The eyes can spot revealing facial expressions and behaviors. The heart can pick up feelings that are not being expressed or that go against the words being said.

Feelings Are as Important as Facts

L et's circle back to feelings again. One of the reasons dogs are such great listeners is that they pay more attention to feelings than to words. Admittedly, that's because they don't understand most of our verbal language, but it's also because they seem to naturally understand that feelings are what matter most when it comes to human beings. Dogs cue in on our feelings. If we're nervous, they become "hyper" and vigilant. If we're content, they flop peacefully by our sides. It is not uncommon for dog lovers to feel that their beloved fur angels understand them better than their spouses or their children do. This is because the dog pays attention to feelings, which humans often miss because they get caught up in the words.

Every human communication has two levels to it: the level of fact and the level of feeling. There's the literal information being communicated and there's the way the person feels about that information. Both are equally important. The facts are conveyed by the words; the feelings are often conveyed nonverbally. Unless you pick up both levels of meaning, you will be woefully in the dark. It's how a person *feels*—passionate, fearful, optimistic—that predicts how he or she is going to behave. And here's an important point to remember: People *want* to be felt, not just heard. They *want* their feelings acknowledged, either expressly or implicitly. This, in fact, is the major way your skill as a listener is measured. Did you pick up the *feelings* being expressed, as well as the facts? The subtler and more complex feelings you are able to detect, the better your listening skills are typically rated and the more "attractive" you are as a listener.

People want to be felt, not just heard.

If you want a fun way to practice reading nonverbal communications, rent a foreign film and watch it without subtitles. See how much of the story you are able to follow. You might be surprised. Sure, you'll miss a lot of the factual details, but you'll probably get the important emotional movements of the film. You'll laugh, you'll cry. You'll notice finer dimensions of the performance you might have missed if you'd had words to rely on.

This is how dogs read us. They may miss a lot of the details, but they follow the major movements of our days and our lives in a more intimate and truthful way than many humans do. Someone recently told me, for example, that she had gone through a difficult period for several days, and her dog never left her side the whole time. None of her friends picked up on her anguish (because she was verbally downplaying it), but her dog was stuck to her hip like Velcro.

The next time you're in a conversation, make a conscious effort to *watch* and *feel*, as much as to hear. You'll be amazed at how much more attuned you are to what's being said. You'll pick up entire dimensions of communication that others miss—except, of course, that fur-covered ball of listening under the table.

Something to
Chew On . . .

If you want to listen like I do, don't *only* pay attention to the words.

Listen for the stuff that's below the words; that's the juicy stuff.

Dogs and humans want to be *felt*, not just heard.

Chaser

Chaser, a border collie, a breed known for their intelligence, lived with John W. Pilley, a retired Wofford College psychology professor. Dr. Pilley read about a dog that had learned to recognize 200 German nouns, so he decided to see if his dog could learn additional words as well. He worked with Chaser for about five hours a day, beginning from the time she was only two months old. Chaser was a quick study and learned to recognize the names of a couple of new objects every day and, eventually, her vocabulary grew to a total of 1,022 nouns!

Chaser got the idea that learning words was her job, and border collies have boundless energy, so Pilley had a hard time taking it easy. He added to their lessons and taught the dog verbs and basic grammar. She came to know more than any other animal of any species except humans. In addition to common nouns like house, ball, and tree, she memorized the names of more than 1,000 toys and could retrieve any of them on command. Based on that learning, she moved on to demonstrate her ability to understand sentences with multiple elements of grammar. Chaser's achievements demonstrate her use of deductive reasoning and complex problem-solving skills to address novel challenges.

Most amazing of all, Chaser isn't unique. John's training methods can be adopted by any dog lover. The book *Chaser: Unlocking the Genius of the Dog Who Knows a Thousand Words*, written by Dr. Pilley and Hilary Hinzmann, shares the story of how John trained Chaser, raised her as a member of the Pilley family, and proved her abilities to the scientific community. It reveals the positive impact of incorporating learning into play and more effectively channeling a dog's natural drives. This is also a wonderful demonstration of a dog's ability to listen with focused intention.

NINE

Always Ready to Play

A dog has lots of friends because he
wags his tail and not his tongue.

—Anonymous

A peculiar thing about dogs and humans: dogs *love* routine. As much as any animal on Earth, dogs seem to relish the predictability of schedules: waking up, eating, doing their business, and going for walks at the same time every day. Repeating the same route through the woods and the streets, sniffing the same bushes and hydrants. Dogs like to know they have a job to do and pride themselves on doing what's expected of them, day after day.

You as a human, on the other hand, probably prefer to see yourself as free-spirited and free-thinking. You downplay your reliance on routine and prefer to point to the unpredictable and autonomous decisions you make. You like to believe you're making free choices and can change your mind on a whim.

But when it comes to spontaneity, who is the real master? Of course, it is the dog. Your dog can be lying on the sofa, snoring away, but if you whisper the words, "Want to go for a walk?" in its ear, it will be off the couch and jumping up and down in a heartbeat. Literally, one physical heartbeat! A dog can be working a bone with single-minded concentration, but if you ask, "Wanna go for a ride?" the bone is *instantly* forgotten. Show a dog a leash, a ball, or a Frisbee, and its entire body will spring to life with the promise of play.

Dogs seem to require almost no transitional period to shift gears. They can go from dead sleep to flying through the air, chasing after a cat in point-zero-three seconds. They don't need to spend half an hour nursing a cup of coffee before they face their day. They don't need to psych themselves up for exercise or wind down before relaxing.

Humans are more likely to resist change. We're not resistant only to *life* change, but also to moment-to-moment change. We get locked in to whatever state we're currently in. If we're in work mode, we have a hard time stopping for a break. Once we're on break, we have a hard time getting back to work. We resist going to sleep at night, but then we can't tear ourselves out of bed in the morning.

Wherever we're at, we want to stay there until *we* feel ready to move on to something new.

The Almighty Agenda

Though you don't consciously realize it, you have an agenda for almost every second of every day. You break your day up into blocks of time and assign each block a purpose. You have dedicated times for exercise, meals, work, fun, spirituality, shopping, and intimacy. You even allot time slots for particular *emotions* and don't feel entirely comfortable mixing them up. There's a time to "be serious" and a time to have fun; a time for action and a time for reflection. Too much laughter at work is unprofessional. Too much heaviness during "Happy Hour"—yes, an hour reserved for being happy—is seen as being a downer.

I was recently struck, for example, by how odd the concept of "comedy" is. Humans literally designate special times for laughing. We go out to a comedy club or watch a comedy on TV so we can enjoy a scheduled period of humor.

When there is no "official" agenda for a given period of the day, you invent one. An agenda for every moment. You don't like it when your spouse wants to talk to you during "catch up on the news" time or when your child asks you probing questions during grocery-shopping or meal-cooking time. You don't want to take calls from your tax attorney when you're watching the game. And you certainly don't want to talk to your mom when you're getting frisky with your mate.

In fact, I would say the number one reason any person is in a bad mood at any given time is that his or her personal agenda was disrupted in some way. We humans, in general, are not good at accepting any change we don't initiate or approve of. Our team loses, our boss yells at us, our date fails to call us back, and we spend the whole day sulking. Some people spend literally years, even entire lifetimes, in a profound state of disappointment because the universe didn't follow their agendas.

Dogs, on the other hand, seem to welcome disruptions to their agendas. They see these as calls to adventure. It's not often a dog will turn down a walk because it is embroiled in a particularly compelling episode of *Jerry Springer Spaniel*. You won't often hear a dog grouse, "It's a little early in the day for my snack," when a meatball is spontaneously offered.

Not only do we assign a purpose to every waking moment, but we also tell ourselves the purpose is tremendously important, and even critical. Humans have a long history of taking themselves too seriously. That's the price we pay, I guess, for having large, abstract, intellectual brains. We tend to live in our heads and to see our thoughts as serious business and critical to functionality of the universe.

Dogs are far humbler and more other-oriented by nature; that's part of the reason for their spontaneity. They don't have any illusions about being masters of the universe and they don't take their own thoughts, agendas, and preferences too seriously. They're willing to go with a new idea, at any time of the day or night (as long as that new idea doesn't involve a trip to the vet).

Being human, you probably feel a sacred duty to remain in control of your own experience and are reluctant to have it hijacked by someone else. However, when you do surrender control and allow the unexpected to happen, you often have the greatest experiences of your life. Odd beings, those humans.

Listening as Play

What does all this have to do with listening? Everything. Because, when you think about it, isn't listening just an invitation to surrender to the unknown? As a listener, you have no real idea what the other person is going to say. You often *think* you do, and that's a problem. To listen well, you must hold yourself in a state of complete openness, ready to receive and respond to whatever shows up. To listen—to *really* listen—means to set all your inner

agendas aside and be prepared to roll
with . . . whatever.

True listening is very much like
play. It requires the same openness
and in-the-moment responsiveness. Listening is like doing impro-
visation instead of learning lines. It's like
jamming instead of playing a rehearsed tune. It's like playing a game
of follow-the-leader in which you're the follower.

**To listen means
to set your inner
agendas aside.**

When we say that an athlete or performer is "in the zone," what
we're really saying is that the person is in the ultimate state of play.
She is responding 100 percent to *what's happening in the moment*.
She is not thinking about the backhand shot she missed a minute
ago or worrying about whether she'll miss the next one. She is totally
focused on what's happening right now and responding only to that.

That's what effective listening is, too.

Listening and play share many of the same qualities and dynamics:

- **Improvisational.** You take your cues from what the other
  "player" is doing, not from what you've got planned in
  your head.
- **Unpredictable.** You don't know what's coming next; it's all
  about alertness and attention.
- **Give and take.** There's a "serve and volley" sort of energy to it.
- **Lack of control.** You don't get to decide ahead of time
  how the game is going to unfold or end. You surrender to
  the game.

- **Total responsiveness.** Like a goalie or a batter, you respond to whatever comes your way from the other party.
- **Present-moment awareness.** You can't be thinking about the past or present; otherwise you'll miss your best play.
- **Challenging.** You need to be on your toes, not lazy or passive.
- **Fun.** It's inherently enjoyable—an adventure, a journey.

And here's perhaps the biggest similarity: to do either of them well—play or listen—you need to be fearless.

The F-Word: Fear

Dogs are always ready to play. They are not fearful of the present moment or of what's to come. They seem to have an inherent faith in the universe and to themselves, a confidence that whatever happens next is going to be okay and they'll be able to deal with it (bath not included). They'll happily jump into the back of a pickup truck with no idea where the truck is going or how long the ride is going to be. They don't know if that truck is headed for Nova Scotia and may never come back; but they're game anyway. Fearless—to a fault, perhaps.

Humans, conversely, are ever fearful about the unknown and about giving up control. We feel anxiety whenever the outcome of a situation is unpredictable, which is why we tend to be poor listeners. The element of the unknown—inherent in listening—pushes our anxiety buttons, and we respond by reverting to familiar, well-worn attitudes and responses.

What Are We Afraid Of?

It may seem odd to bring up fear when we talk about listening, but I believe that most of our poor listening habits really do spring from fear. Not abject terror, of course, but anxiety. Worry. Discomfort. Nervousness. We feel a little edgy every time someone tells us that we have to stop and listen. We are suddenly required to focus when we didn't plan to. It's a loss of control. This causes our brains to react with a solution that provides quick relief, such as interrupting, mentally rehearsing, zoning out, or any of the other leash-law violations. Anxiety is one reason that we aren't beautiful, doglike listeners.

What is it about the experience of surrendering our attention to another human being that causes anxiety? Here are a few of the more common fears:

We're worried we'll have to set our own agenda aside. One of our biggest conversational fears is that if we allow the other person to have the floor, their agenda will steal the show and we won't be able to say what *we* wanted to say. If you're making a sales call, for example, you're afraid you might lose the opportunity to sell your products. In a relationship conversation, perhaps you fear that if the other person gets on a soapbox first, your point of view will be squeezed out.

Well, guess what? Maybe it will; deal with it. Seriously! Let your agenda go. Give your full attention to someone else's. It's a give-and-ye-shall-receive type thing. The person will be so appreciative of your generous listening, you *will* be given the chance to make your case, either later in this conversation or in a later conversation, *and* you will become known as a caring listener.

We're afraid of being criticized. Often when someone tells you they want to talk to you, you are afraid they're going to take you to task in some way. So you go on the defensive, consciously or unconsciously. You brace for criticism before it even happens. You mentally scramble to defend yourself and are no longer really listening to what the other person has to say.

In most cases, your fear is unfounded. But even when the other person *does* wish to criticize you, the most powerful thing you can do is to simply listen, openly and non-defensively, resisting all urges to defend yourself.

This accomplishes two things. First of all, it defuses the other person's issue. By simply listening, without self-defending, you disarm the critic and dissipate their "attack" energy, in much the same way that jiu jitsu absorbs the power of a physical attack. Second, by showing that you are willing to listen openly and non-defensively to criticism, you cement your reputation as an exceptional listener and make a quantum leap in trust with that person. When people discover they can talk to you, about *you*, they know they can talk to you about anything.

We're afraid of getting sucked into a conversational "black hole." One of our biggest fears when a person starts talking is that the conversation is going to blossom into a major time-and-attention suck. We worry that we're going to have to give up a precious chunk of our day, so we signal reluctance, impatience, or irritation to the other person. Communication is stifled.

I've discovered that open, caring listening is more efficient. What might have taken sixty minutes if you listened distractedly gets done in ten. Of course, sometimes the issue on the table is, indeed, a time-consuming one. In that case you can simply say something like, "What you're telling me is important, and I want to make sure I give it enough attention. I only have a few minutes right now, but let's find a time we can talk about this in more detail."

We're afraid of wandering into a conversational landmine. Whenever someone wants to talk to you, especially in private, there's a possibility the conversation is going to take you someplace you don't want to go. The speaker might want to talk about something overly confidential, something squirm-inducing, or something that puts you in a no-win position (e.g., a girlfriend asking, "Do you think this dress makes me look fat?" or a boyfriend asking, "So, do you like my mom?").

That's not a good reason to put up listening walls, though. If you sense a conversational red flag popping up, you certainly have a right (and a duty, really) to hit the stop button. Think of it as an opportunity to demonstrate good character. By drawing clear lines about what you will or will not listen to (e.g., gossip or slander), and by admitting honestly when you feel your attention is being misused, your stock will go up, not down. You will gain a reputation as someone who listens openly, but who also has boundaries and a good moral compass.

We're afraid we're going to be "recruited." Another major fear in listening is that we're going to be asked to do something we don't want to do or give something we don't want to give. This is true both at home and the office. After all, when a boss or coworker asks to talk to you, there's a better than 50 percent chance that your time, allegiance, or labor is being sought.

We're afraid we're not going to have answers. Another common fear we have in listening is that we're not going to have the answers/solutions/expertise we feel we're supposed to have. Thus, much of the time when we should be listening, we're actually mentally trying to find a way to be the answer person.

This fear of not knowing the answer is an impediment to playfulness and spontaneity.

Humility: The Power of "I Don't Know"

Early in my career, I had an embarrassing moment that stuck with me and taught me a great deal. I was spending the day with my boss's boss's boss, a visiting VP. We were conducting some in-person meetings out in the field. Early in the day he asked me a question that I felt I should have known the answer to, but didn't.

Worried about appearing unprepared and inexpert, I spun an elaborate concoction of bull excrement. Though I thought I had gotten away with it, my little fiction-writing exercise ate at me for the rest of the day.

Sure enough, when the VP and I were parting company at day's end, he praised my work but said, "One thing, though. When you don't know the answer to a question, it's better to just say, 'I don't know, but I'll find out and get back to you.'" My face turned fifty shades of crimson, I'm sure. His words burrowed into my gut.

Since that day I have taken the VP's advice to heart and have been continually astounded by the magical power of the simple words, "I don't know." Showing vulnerability, I've learned, is not a flaw or a sign of weakness, but a wonderful asset.

The fact is, when people talk to you, their main desire is to be heard and understood, not necessarily to have their problems fixed or their questions answered. Solutions can come later. The main thing, *right now*, is to understand. An attitude of "I may not know the answer but I want to hear your concerns" keeps you humble, open, and receptive. People would rather think you understand them and are *working* on a solution than that you are jumping in with solutions without really hearing them. Humility opens far more doors than infallibility.

Dogs are beautifully humble creatures. They don't take themselves too seriously. They are willing to "take one for the team" and let you treat them in embarrassing ways (ballet tutu for the family bulldog, anyone?); yet they remain noble in spite of this— perhaps *because* of this.

Humility opens far more doors than infallibility.

The paradoxical thing I've discovered is that people actually respect you *more* when you lose your pretentions of omniscience. They begin to trust you, knowing that when you *do* give them a confident answer, they can depend on it. Why? Because when you *don't* know, you admit it. Conversely, those who posture themselves as know-it-alls are not trustworthy, because their need to look smart trumps their need to be honest. And others know that.

Getting over yourself and being humble opens up the spirit of play in all of your interactions with others.

Reframing Anxiety as Excitement

Our fears and anxieties are what keep us from a state of play. Here's something to keep in mind about anxiety, though. Neuroscience tells us that anxiety and excitement are essentially the same physiological state. Both involve stress and an increase in adrenaline, but we perceive one as negative (anxiety) and the other as positive (excitement). I find it's often possible (and this is echoed by Laurie Mintz in her article in *Psychology Today*, "Beating the Odds: Reframing Anxiety as Excitement")[36] to mentally flip a situation of anxiety into one of excitement. After all, they're basically the same state. Only our attitude *toward* the state is different.

What I'm suggesting is that we can transform the mild sense of anxiety we feel when asked to listen to another person into a sense of adventure—of play, of fun—like that dog jumping into the back of a pickup truck even though he has no idea where it's going. When we expect the best instead of anticipating the worst, many of our conversations become more exciting, fun, and stimulating.

Playing Well with Others

A doglike spirit of play works magic when speaking to groups. And interactivity (i.e., listening) is the key that turns it on.

When most of us are communicating, especially with a group, we tend to be more comfortable with prepared material. We often plan

36 http://www.psychologytoday.com/blog/stress-and-sex/201108/beating-the-odds-reframing-anxiety -excitement

every beat of a presentation, right down to the dumb little jokes we're going to tell. It doesn't even occur to us to engage in a meaningful dialogue with the audience—after all, that could derail our entire planned presentation. So after a few little surface interactions, like "Hey, how's everybody doing today?" or asking everyone's name and job title, we go right into our canned stuff.

What I've discovered is that the less I *lecture* and the more I interact with my audience, the better my presentation goes—without fail. When I'm interactive, the audience stays alive, engaged, and awake, from start to finish.

Typically I bring along the standard PowerPoint slideshow as a backup. I'll tell the audience, right up front, "I brought thirty-two slides, which I'm happy to share with you, but I'd really rather hear what *you'd* like to talk about." It may take some prodding to get the first response or two, but then, usually, the floodgates open. The suggestions and comments start flying. I'm already listening and improvising.

When I'm working this way—or should I say, *playing* this way—the time often flies by and we enjoy a presentation based on information they want to hear rather than stuff I want to say. The feedback is usually positive. It's not because I'm such a gifted speaker; it's really just that I make the effort to engage the audience: to take in what they say and to respond to them genuinely, not just as a way to segue back to my script.

They come to listen, but instead they themselves are listened *to*— what a novel concept!

Improv Mode Versus Performance Mode

A good friend of mine did stand-up comedy some years back, and he told me about a painful night when he had to go on stage after one of the most brilliant performances he had ever seen. Paula Poundstone was just beginning her set when she was distracted by the shoes of an audience member in the front row. Instead of ignoring the shoes, she made a joke about them.

The audience member responded to her, and she got into a dialogue with him. Then another audience member in the back of the room made a remark, and she brought him into the act, creating an impromptu dialogue between the two men. This went on and on as she invented an absurd story about the two of them and the shoes, weaving in the live commentary of other audience members. In her entire twenty minutes, she didn't do a single line of prepared material! My friend tells me the audience was laughing so hard, they were literally falling off their chairs. When Poundstone's set ended, she received a two-minute standing ovation.

The reason the audience was so appreciative of Poundstone, of course, was that she'd had the presence to take in what she was being given in the moment, use it, and trust her natural humor gifts to shine. The result was an improvisational masterpiece that never could have happened if she'd stuck to the script.

There are two basic modes you can be in when communicating: "performance" mode or "improv" mode. When you're in "performance" mode, you're the star of a one-person show, but when you're in "improv" mode, you make the people around you your costars.

"Performing," I've learned, is often about feeding your ego or catering to your fears. Improv is more humble and listening-driven. It brings others into the act, and both the performers and the audience are enriched and energized. Of course, sometimes you *need* to use prepared material, but whenever the situation allows, start practic-

Accepting input during your scheduled output will often serve you well.

ing being more improvisational. Preparation is always warranted, but learning to listen (e.g., accepting input) during your scheduled session of output, will most often serve you well.

A few tips I've picked up for playing improv with an audience:

- **Breathe.** Anytime you're feeling disconnected from an audience, just look them in the eye and take a long, deep breath. Imagine that you are literally breathing their presence into you. Nothing centers you and brings you back to the present moment like breathing.
- **Ask for feedback from the audience often.** Then listen to, and *use*, the feedback you're given, in a meaningful, substantive way.
- **Breathe.**
- **Welcome surprises.** Surprises and miscues are your friends. *Use* them; don't fear or ignore them. Whatever goofs happen, make them part of your "act." Don't ignore them.
- **Breathe.**

- **Let gifted audience members shine.** Many speakers fear having an audience member who is funnier or cleverer than they are. That's pure ego. I love it when there's a funny or outspoken person in the group. Far from diminishing me, it enhances my presentation greatly by providing me with new material.
- **Breathe.**

Playing One-on-One

Slipping into "performance" (versus improvisational) mode can be just as much a danger when you're talking one-on-one as it is when talking to a group. We've all been forced to listen to salespeople and others who dump pre-rehearsed performances on us. They might as well be talking to a mannequin. Most of us have also been guilty of that ourselves—putting on a show that doesn't really include the other person.

This is a wasted opportunity. Sitting right across the table from you, or talking on the phone with you, is a living, breathing person who would prefer to be engaged with you than to just sit there trying to download the content you're spewing out. Why not embrace that opportunity? True, you may have to give up some of your scripted gems, but what you gain in return is immeasurably richer—an actual *dialogue*. A connection is made, and that connection is far more valuable than anything you were prepared to say.

Instead of being fearful that listening to others is going to throw you off your game or preempt your agenda, *welcome* every question or comment as an opportunity to play, to improvise, to explore. Take inspiration from dogs, and be ready to "jump into the back of the pickup truck" at a moment's notice. Trust that your instincts will almost always take you to a more intriguing place than a memorized script will. No matter what agenda you *think* is so earth-shatteringly important, forming connections with the people around you is always more important; every dog knows that. And connections happen only when you give up the idea that your script is going to play out the way you wrote it in your head.

And know that the pickup truck will safely bring you back home again.

Something to
Chew On . . .

Listening is like play; you've got to stay in the moment!

I never pretend to know *stuff*, and people love me for it.

Humans are a lot like me; they want attention, not answers.

Rowan

Rowan is a German Spitz from England who was born without eyes. The victim of a congenital defect, Rowan has been blind his entire life, but strangers meeting him rarely notice. Rowan can run and catch and navigate his way through the world as well as any dog who can see, matching them step for step. He does it by listening.

To "see," Rowan barks, and uses the echo that follows to piece together the shape of the world around him. What he does is a type of echolocation, the same thing bats use to be able to fly at night. They emit a sound too high-pitched for humans to hear, and when the sound echoes back, the subtle changes in pitch and strength tell them what the sound wave bounced off of.

Dogs don't use echolocation, but without eyes Rowan, at a young age, was forced to teach himself how to create a mental map by comparing the different echoes the sound created when he barked. He became so finely attuned to this way of seeing that he's even aware of when trees lose their leaves for winter, a fact that eventually tipped off his owners to what he was doing.

Rowan's owner, Sam Orchard, said, "People who meet Rowan can't tell that he's blind at first. They usually just ask why he's got his eyes shut. When he was born five days early I kept waiting for him to open his eyes, and when he didn't I took him to the vet. It was a real surprise when he told me that not only would they not be opening, they didn't exist. He was born without eyes. I was shocked, but I decided that I would just do the best I could for him, and now he is just like the others, only a bit more special."

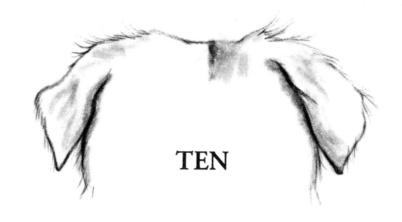

TEN

The Herd (Heard) Effect

So much of language is unspoken.
So much of language is comprised of looks
and gestures and sounds that are not words.
People are ignorant of the vast complexity
of their own communication.

—Enzo (the dog), *The Art of Racing*
in the Rain by Garth Stein

I've spent a lot of time urging you to "zip it"—to embrace silence and quell the urge to make unnecessary noise from your mouth. While I can't overstate how important that is, I don't want to create the impression that listening is all about being still; it's not. There are many *active* things a good listener must do to keep a conversation moving forward. Once again, you-know-who leads the pack.

One of the most remarkable qualities of dogs is their ability to herd: to guide other creatures (especially humans) to where they need to go and to prevent them from wandering off the trail. But it's the *way* they do it that really impresses; dogs somehow manage to follow and lead at the same time.

Dogs' herding talents can be most easily observed by watching actual herding dogs, such as border collies, corgis or Australian shepherds. A herding dog is able to figure out where the herd of sheep needs to go and to gently—or sometimes *not* so gently—guide the creatures to their destination. As long as the animals are on the right path, the dog just flanks the herd, remaining alert and watchful. But as soon as the sheep start to stray, the dog steps in and becomes more assertive, guiding them in the desired direction.

This herding ability is also on display when a dog goes for a walk with a human. I'm talking about an off-leash walk where it's just you and your dog, out on the trails. If you're lucky enough to live in an area where you can free-walk with a dog like this and not be busy barking orders, you'll notice that the dog does a masterful job of both following and leading you. First it tries to figure out where you want to go. It "reads" you—your eyes, your posture, your head movements, your voice, even your mood. (And of course, if you've walked a particular route in the past, the dog will remember it.) Once it has an idea where you want to go, it works at gently keeping you on track. Like an effective server in a restaurant who doesn't make his presence known until the customer needs something, the dog hovers near you unobtrusively, keeping an eye on both you and the trail. If you appear confused, it will trot ahead and show you the way. If you slow down or stop for too long, it will encourage you to get moving. If you start to take a wrong turn, it will show you the correct route.

The dog is content to let *you* choose the destination and even the preferred route for getting there, but the moment you seem to lose direction or momentum, it is there to gently put you back on track: not to where *it* wants you to go, but to where *you* want to go.

Why do dogs do this? Perhaps it has to do with the fact that they are pack animals and want the pack to remain together. It's in their nature. They seem happiest when everyone is together and "on the same page." The pack also represents safety. The safety in numbers concept is something that most humans experience themselves as well.

Whatever the motivation, herding is a masterful ability, one that no other animal does better. It's one that humans would do well to learn.

In many ways, being a good listener is like being a good herder. Your job is to pay close attention to the speaker and to try to get a sense as to where he is going and what his goal is. As long as he seems to be getting there on his own, you allow him to take the lead, just giving him little signs now and then that you're with him. But the moment you realize he has taken a wrong turn, run out of steam, or gotten a bit lost, you step in and gently steer him back.

An effective herder forms the habit of making sure the group is all together before allowing a conversation to barrel ahead to new places.

Herding. Or maybe we should call it "heard"-ing.

An effective herder first makes sure the group is all together.

To Herd or Not to Herd

W hen I talk about herding in conversation, I mean all the cues you give as a listener to help the speaker stay on track. Herding can include everything from gentle nods of the head to extensive questioning and prodding of the person speaking—whatever is required to prevent the speaker from wandering into the brambles. The amount of herding you choose to do in a given situation depends on several factors:

Your role. Your responsibility to herd the speaker depends greatly on the role you are playing at that moment. Certain roles permit—and require—a lot of herding; others do not. If you are a meeting facilitator or debate moderator, for example, you have a high responsibility to herd the speaker(s). If you are simply a meeting attendee, audience member, or invited guest, your role in herding the speaker is much more limited.

The number of people present. Generally speaking, the more listeners present, the less individual responsibility (and permission) you have to herd. As the size of the listening group shrinks, though, your herding role increases. In a one-on-one situation, it becomes your sole responsibility to lead the speaker through the woods and get him home.

Your relationship with the speaker. Your herding powers are also constrained, to a large extent, by your relationship with the speaker. You must have status with a speaker in order to herd him. As a general rule, the higher the position and authority of the speaker relative to the listener, the longer the "leash" you must grant before trying to rein him in. It's doubtful you will try to put a leash on the president of your company when listening to him.

The need for herding. Of course, the amount of herding you do depends on the amount of herding *needed.* A speaker who is effectively delivering his or her message requires very little herding, except for occasional nods. A speaker who is lost, unfocused, or prone to wandering off the path every time he or she is offered a distraction may need constant herding.

The importance of the message. As a herder, you need to pick your battles. You don't need to get exact clarity on every minor point the speaker is making, but you do need clarity on the biggies. If the speaker's most important messages are not being expressed well, then you *must* herd, herd, and herd some more.

Your commitment to listen. Ultimately, the amount of herding you do comes down to the strength of your commitment to listen. How committed are you to understanding what the speaker has to say? Are you willing to work at it?

If you are committed to listening to what others have to say, you will become a dedicated herder. That doesn't mean you will interrupt the speaker unnecessarily, but it does mean that, just like a dog, you will herd the speaker back onto the trail when he or she wanders off.

Levels of Herding

There are several levels of herding or feedback that may be employed. In my view, herding falls into three basic intensity levels: (1) simple guidance, (2) reflective checking in, and (3) active

pulling. Each one calls for very different behaviors on the part of
the herder.

1. Simple Guidance

This is the base level of herding that is required of almost
all listeners in almost all listening situations. It is analogous
to the subtle signals a dog sends you when it's out on the trail
with you. Every now and then the dog will look at you, make
eye contact, and maybe give you a little shake of the tail or a
smile, just to let you know it is "with" you and everything is
going fine. Similarly, when listening, you have a responsibility
to periodically let speakers know they're doing fine (assuming
they *are* doing fine), that you're receiving their message, and
that no course corrections are warranted.

Herding at this level can entail things like:

- Nodding
- Making eye contact
- Keeping an alert, attentive posture
- Taking notes
- Laughing as appropriate
- Changing your facial expression to reflect the emo-
  tional content of the speech
- Moving forward in your seat to receive key messages

These simple, encouraging actions are hugely important
for the speaker. In their absence, the speaker begins to feel
anxiety: *Have I wandered off course? Am I losing my listener(s)?*

Is my listener off in Aspen with their fantasy lover? Am I being unclear? Have I said something offensive?

Of course, sometimes the speaker *has* gone astray, and you need to let him know. Sometimes the speaker is lacking confidence due to the subject matter, the situation, or your responses, or lack thereof. This is where supportive herding behaviors on your part, as the listener, come into play. Encouragement and even leading with your invisible leash can be greatly appreciated.

2. Reflective Checking In

At the next level of herding, your feedback becomes much more proactive and tailored to the person speaking. You play an active role in making sure the speaker is fully expressing himself and that you are fully understanding him. Reflective checking in is employed at select times during conversations—for example, when you sense that the speaker really needs to feel heard, when *you* really need to be clear on what the speaker is saying, or when you want to create a more supportive bond with the speaker.

To listen reflectively is a well-established concept in listening circles; I certainly didn't make it up. It simply means to reflect back to the speaker what he just said. This isn't something we should do all the time—that would come off as a little strange and terribly annoying—but it is definitely an important skill to add to our listening repertoire. Reflective checking in can take several forms.

Simple repetition. Sometimes simply repeating back, verbatim, what the speaker just said—perhaps adding "I hear you," "I see," or "I understand" to it—is all that's needed. This simple type of statement, though not very creative or personalized, effectively lets the person know you are hearing what is being said. So, if a customer comes in and says, "I'm really upset with the way I was treated by one of your employees," you might just say, "I understand that you're upset by the way you were treated." Don't argue; don't try to fix it. Just reflect, like a mirror.

This technique is often used in couples' therapy. In my opinion it could be effectively employed in a much wider range of settings, such as the workplace, the home, and the political arena. (But can you teach an old dog a new trick?) All too often *deflection* is the method used in these settings, leading to longer-term issues.

Repetition in new words. Though simple repetition can be effective, it gets old and becomes annoying pretty fast if you keep using it, for example:

"I'm dissatisfied with the service I've gotten."

"I understand you're dissatisfied with the service you've gotten."

"I'm hoping you can do something about it."

"You're hoping I can do something about it."

"Boy, you're really starting to annoy me."

"What I hear you saying is that I'm really starting to annoy you."

A higher form of reflection is to repeat back what the person said by paraphrasing. This tends to sound more natural upset that the package didn't come on time. You're probably feeling a little misled at this point." Or perhaps by stating your own feelings: "I get that you're angry the package was late, and I'm disappointed in our company for letting you down." Sometimes it's also helpful to add a promise or action step of some kind: "I know you're worried that the package won't come in time for the holidays, and I'm sorry we put you in this position. I want to correct this right now."

It's not about making the conversation revolve around you; it's about adding a supportive personal element to what the other person said. This shows that you not only heard the other person but also absorbed their message and were somehow moved by it.

When you're sad or unhappy, a dog doesn't go fetch the leash, trying to force its agenda on you; it gives you a lick on the face, letting you know it not only understands what you're feeling but also cares: empathy with a tail. Then it gets the leash, but how can we blame them!

3. Active Pulling

Finally, if you are a committed listener, there will be times when you'll need to go beyond simple guidance and reflective checking in. You will need to become the active puller in the conversation, extracting more information than the speaker may be volunteering. I'm not necessarily talking about adversarial situations, such as grilling a crime suspect; I mean those times when the speaker is reluctant, guarded, shut down, or

than rote repetition. For example, you might say, "So t|
service wasn't up to your expectations," or, "Something we'v
done has let you down." This demonstrates a more authen|
tic level of understanding than trying to be a human tape
recorder: you've grasped the message enough to restate it in
your own words.

Emotional reflection. An even more effective form of reflection is one that also recognizes the speaker's emotional state.
"I understand the product you ordered didn't come on time,
and you seem worried about that." Or: "You think I acted self-
ishly, and that hurts your feelings."
Remember, we live in our
emotions, and we want to
be *understood* at that level.
So if a listener not only
appears to understand *what*
you've said but *how you feel*
about it, a whole new level of trust

We live in our emotions and want to be understood there.

opens up. It's important, however, not to allow your emotions
to unconsciously reflect those of the speaker. Sometimes when
someone is angry, for example, it is easy to respond in anger.
This is not usually helpful.

Reflection with a personal twist. Perhaps the highest form
of reflection occurs when you not only feed back an understanding of the speaker's message and feelings but also add
perspective of your own. This can be expressed in several ways.
Perhaps by supplying a bit of interpretation: "I can see you're

simply unaware that he may have more to say on the matter at hand. Active pulling requires a high level of commitment as a listener. It means that you are truly invested in understanding the other person and are willing to "go digging" in order to improve that understanding.

Run-of-the-mill listeners avoid active pulling; it's too much work. Besides, you might annoy the speaker or hear something you don't want to hear. It's far easier to just take the speaker at face value. But if you want to become a first-rate listener, active pulling must be in your arsenal. If you sense there is an unspoken message hiding below the surface, sometimes you must go after it.

To become a first-rate listener, active pulling must be in your arsenal.

Ultimately, *you* become the beneficiary of your own active pulling. You clear the air of unspoken thoughts and feelings around you. This frees you from the negative consequences of those hidden feelings. Think about it: would you rather find out *why* your spouse feels hurt, or live with three days of one-word answers and slammed doors? Would you rather find out *why* your boss no longer confides in you, or allow his unspoken feelings to derail your career?

By active pulling, you keep the channels of communication around you clear. You check in with people to make sure there are no unspoken issues. You take the emotional temperature around you and try to address problems before they harden into negativity. You don't accept a sullen "Nothing" in answer to the question, "What's wrong?" You dig, you prod, you check under the hood. You're not afraid to play amateur therapist.

A journalist is a professional puller. Journalists get their interview subjects to open up about their experiences and feelings. Doing so, of course, provides a more compelling interview or broadcast segment for readers and television audiences. Journalists will ask certain certain types of questions, each of which is an example of active pulling:

Open-ended versus closed-ended questions. A closed-ended question is one that is basically informational in nature and requires only a one-word answer, for example: "What's in the shopping bag?" An open-ended question is one that requires a more expansive response, such as: "How did you like shopping at that new store?"

A closed-ended question from a doctor to a patient, for example, might be, "Do you have any major health issues you want to tell me about?" Many patients simply answer no to this; conversation over. An open-ended way to ask the question might be, "Tell me about your biggest health concern at the moment." This assumes the patient has *some* health concerns (everyone does), and encourages more honest sharing.

Most of us have been taught, or know from experience, that asking open-ended questions is more effective than asking closed-ended ones. Then why don't we do it more often? Harsh as this may sound, I think it's because we really don't want to invest the time and effort in listening to another person's perspective. We'd rather load the question so as to get the answer *we* want to hear.

Feeling questions. Questions like, "How do you feel about that?" and, "Why do you feel so strongly about this?" are effective and get to the core of the matter quickly. There's a good reason for this. *Feeling* questions, by nature, get to the heart of an issue and invite thoughtful, expansive responses. In business situations, we tend to stick to informational questions. And yet feelings lie at the heart of most decision-making, even in business. I'm not suggesting that you should turn business meetings into therapy sessions, but it is crucial to learn how customers, team members, employees, supervisors, and others *feel* about new initiatives, products, and personnel. Why? Because feelings dictate behavior.

Leading questions. These questions are intended to land someone on a particularly fruitful topic. We are taught how to use them, particularly in sales, and the skilled communicator understands their value. "How do you feel about seeing your ex this Christmas?" is probably a more productive question than, "Are you enjoying the holidays?" In a business environment, "How are the budget cuts impacting the new project?" beats a simple, "How's it going?" because it encourages the employee to focus on an issue that is likely causing him some concerns.

There are two kinds of leading questions: the type designed to get the answer you want to hear, and the type designed to help people open up about an area of *their* concern.

Which do you suppose I recommend?

Sleeping Dogs?

A good herder sometimes leads others where they don't want to go.

Being a good herder some-times means leading people to places they don't even want to go themselves. To do this, you must be willing to deal with negative energy.

Often the reason some people are reticent about a topic is that they are feeling resentful, angry, or blameful about it. They may not feel it is safe or appropriate to voice these negative feelings. To encourage them to speak openly is to risk having them dump their negativity on you, and that is no fun. Much of the reason people don't engage in active pulling, I think, is that they don't want to wake sleeping dogs. Better to let them lie.

But *is* it better, really? I find that by getting negative energy on the table as early as possible, you defuse it before it has a chance to metastasize into long-term resentment. Healthy, mature couples, for example, learn to express their disagreements as soon as they arise, then move on. They don't let small issues fester into big ones. Less mature couples, however, may strive to "keep the peace" at all costs, failing to state their disagreements openly. In these relationships, there are often smoldering veins of resentment that poison the air over time and drive a wedge between the partners.

Paradoxically, *avoiding* negative emotions actually brings more of them into your life. People who don't like talking about "nega-tive" things end up holding on to their negative energy rather than releasing it. They deny feeling bad, but they express it in other ways.

Ask yourself: would a dog do this? If you pulled a dog's tail or bothered a dog while it was eating, would the dog smile bitterly at you and say, "Everything's fine"? No, it would snap at you or give you a sharp bark, right away, to let you know it was not pleased with you.

Dogs don't carry negative energy around. You never feel like the mood just got heavy because a dog walked into the room. Quite the opposite, actually. Dogs carry clean energy because they express their negative impulses the moment they occur.

Listener Prep

In today's listening-challenged world, it's not enough to be good listeners ourselves. You must empower *others* to listen better to you. "Listener prep" is something I find myself doing more and more these days. By that I mean setting up the listener to do a better job of listening by establishing clear *goals and expectations* for the conversation.

If I make a business phone call, for example, I might say something like this after the initial pleasantries have been exchanged: "I want to share a funny story with you. After that, I'm going to explain to you why the story is relevant to the goals we're trying to accomplish. Then, if you don't mind, I want to ask your opinion on an important related matter. The whole thing should take about five to ten minutes. Do you have time now or should I call back at a better time?"

It may seem oddly artificial to "set up" a conversation ahead of time like that, but it can be immensely beneficial in many ways. First of all, it tells the other person how to orient their brain right from the start. In an average conversation, you often have no idea what the other person's agenda is. You end up spending half the conversation trying to figure out why the person is talking to you and how long it's going to take. Meanwhile, you're not really listening to the person. However, when the other person *tells* you what his goals and expectations are, you know what to expect, so you can lower your anxiety. Remember, people love clear expectations.

Offering the listener an estimated time frame for the conversation lowers the anxiety level even more, because now the person no longer has to worry about the talk turning into an unwelcome gabfest that is going to eat up half his afternoon. Even if it is going to be a long conversation, by offering him a heads-up about it, you at least give him a choice in the matter. By agreeing to continue the conversation, he is giving you his commitment to listen.

Preparing a listener is like showing a dog a ball before you get in the car to go to the park. Now the dog knows what to expect and can eagerly anticipate a game of fetch (and behave accordingly).

Telling others your expectations of *them* helps them to better play the listening role you require. Most people don't automatically know what role to play. Should they be leading or following? Making a joke? Offering an opinion? Just keeping their mouths shut? It helps to be told. For example, when I call a friend, I often preface the conversation by saying something like, "I need to talk something out with you; I'm not looking for advice," or, if I do need advice, I might say, "I really need your help sorting something out." Some of my friends do this with me, too. It's a big help because it tells you, as the listener, how to be most useful and supportive to the other person. It takes off the pressure to play Yoda when the person only wants an ear. On the other hand it cues you to listen more critically if you know your advice is wanted.

Teaching others about the kind of listening you want at any given time may be the best herding of all. This is another great thing about dogs as listeners, no instruction or coaching is necessary.

Supporting the Speaker

You can do the same sort of thing for the speaker when it's your turn to listen. Simply ask the speaker how you can best serve him or her. At the beginning of a conversation, if I'm going to serve primarily as the listener, I might ask, "How can I best help you? Would you like me to just listen or are you hoping for some feedback?" *Help me help you* is the theme I try to communicate. When you ask speakers what kind of listening they want, *they* become much more focused in their communication, right from the get-go.

Help me help you is the theme I try to communicate.

As the conversation unfolds, you can further support the speaker by periodically announcing what you're up to on the listening end. When I've been listening silently to another person on the phone for a while, for instance, I might say, "I'm just trying to take in everything you're sharing; that's why I'm not saying much." This helps lower the anxiety level in the speaker. He or she knows my quietness isn't because

I'm texting my buddies about tonight's big game, but because I'm listening carefully.

Managing Role Shifts

In most conversations, the roles of listener and speaker shift from time to time. You may be the speaker for a while, then you're the listener, then the speaker again—back and forth. Again, it can be helpful to announce these shifts explicitly, so that both of you feel adequately heard and are on the same page. I'll often say things like, "I want to respond to what you just said, but first I want to make sure you've said everything you want to say," or, "I just have one more point to make, then I want to be quiet and hear what you have to say." Making the expectations clear allows you to shift back and forth between speaking and listening roles without fearing you're being rude or presumptuous or cutting the other person off before they've had their complete say.

Setting Limits

Sometimes your role as a herder is to rein in the speaker—like a dog that must keep a sheep from walking off a cliff, even if that means giving it a nip on the heel.

Let's face it: some speakers can be obnoxious, unfocused, unprepared, and/or inconsiderate. They may carry on about meaningless minutiae, insult or bore their audience, and/or wander from topic to topic with no discernible sense of direction. Sometimes, for the sake of the clock or the sanity of others, including yourself, you must get the speaker to *stop*, for the love of God (or Dog), and change course. Breaking off eye contact, looking around the room, and turning your body slightly away are some subtle, semi-polite ways to do this. But sometimes actively interrupting is necessary. Sometimes you just need to put up a big ol' stop sign.

Being a good listener does not mean being a doormat. Part of good listening is being a *critical* listener, and if the other person stubbornly refuses to make a point, you must let him know that your time and attention are valuable.

After you've made a few subtle attempts to herd the speaker onto a more productive trail, there is nothing wrong with politely curtailing the conversation or asking the speaker to get back on track. You may suggest something like, "Why don't you go back to your earlier point, since it seemed important to you."

The Finish Line

Finally, one of the most important herding steps you can take is to let the speaker know if and when she has reached her destination. When it becomes clear that she's said everything she needs to say—perhaps she begins repeating herself or lapsing into filler comments—you can show her that she has successfully "made it home" by summing up what she said in an accurate, insightful manner. Summing up not only puts a punctuation mark on the speaker's output, but also gives the speaker confidence that you have received the message fully and completely.

You may even wish to propose action steps for moving forward. Proposing action steps is the best way to show that you have fully grasped the speaker's message. Not only do you *understand* it, but you have internalized it to the point where you can confidently state what needs to happen next, and you care enough to play an active part in making that next step happen.

Something to
Chew On . . .

I love it when you show me the ball before we go to the park. It tells me we're going to play, not going to the doctor. People like to know what to expect in conversations, too.

Herding doesn't mean making people go where *you* want them to go; it means helping them get to where *they* want to go.

Sometimes when a speaker won't make his point, you've just got to bark and say, "Enough's enough," and safely guide him.

Nipper

One of the most iconic images of the twentieth century was the famous logo of Nipper, the RCA dog, listening intently to a gramophone horn, often accompanied by the words, "His Master's Voice." If a picture is worth a thousand words, then Nipper's must be worth 10 million—capturing the essence of listening itself. Is it a coincidence that the most universal symbol for listening uses a dog as its subject and not a human?

The real Nipper lived in Bristol, England, in the late 1800s, and was a mixed-breed who got his name because he would bite the backs of visitors' legs (probably because they were talking too much). After the passing of his original owner, Mark Henry Barraud, Nipper went to live with Henry's brothers, Philip and Francis. Nipper passed away several years later but left a big impression on Francis, who painted a picture of Nipper intently listening to a wind-up cylinder phonograph. Francis eventually sold the painting to The Gramophone Company, which later became RCA. The rest is advertising history, and the iconic image became an international symbol of quality and excellence for the brand.

The artist, Francis Barraud, said, "It is difficult to say how the idea came to me beyond that fact that it suddenly occurred to me that to have my dog listening to the phonograph, with an intelligent and rather puzzled expression, and call it 'His Master's Voice' would make an excellent subject. We had a phonograph and I often noticed how puzzled he was to make out where the voice came from. It certainly was the happiest thought I ever had." [37]

Nipper's iconic image can even be found in statuary from Japan to New York, including an enormous four-ton Nipper that sits atop a building in Albany. The way we listen to our music might change, but listening like a dog never goes out of fashion.

---

37 Rolfs, Joan & Robin. (2007). Nipper Collectibles, The RCA Victor Trademark Dog. Audio Antique LLC, USA.

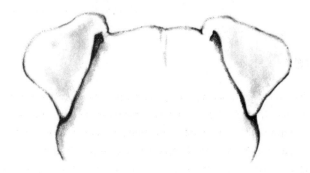

Making
Your
Mark

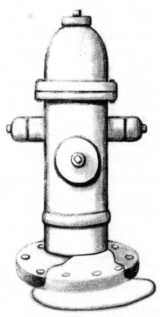

In order to really enjoy a dog,
one doesn't merely try to train him
to be semi-human. The point of it is to
open oneself to the possibility of
becoming partly a dog.

—Edward Hoagland

Early on, I said that the goal of listening is to understand. That is true. But if you want to listen like a dog you can't ignore the element of service. From Yukon Bob, an Alaskan malamute getting ready to harness up for the Iditarod, to Roamy, a mixed breed fur angel burrowed next to his master during a cold, rainy night, dogs know about service. They even seem to know that listening itself is a service. For example, Tiger Woods reportedly suffered from a stuttering problem as a child. He talked to his dog every night as a way to overcome it.

Listening Is Service

Perhaps a dog's most extraordinary quality of all is its incredible service-mindedness. Dogs seem to live to serve. And it's us they seem intent on serving. They pull our sleds. They track down criminals, and find lost people. They guide our blind. They guard our crops and cattle. They fight alongside us on the battlefield. They aid our physically disabled. They have been our friends and confidants. They love us like no other. They even teach us to be better people through their love, loyalty, and courage. And in return they have asked for very little. A walk. A treat. Your love.

You might think serving others means giving up ground or losing control. But you'll find the opposite can be true. You can actually lead better as a listener. In his book *The One Minute Manager*, Ken Blanchard says the secret to improving both productivity and job satisfaction involves taking just that one minute to stop, listen, hear, and understand those being managed. Clearly Blanchard believes in the power of service, as another of his books carries the title *The Servant Leader.*

In short: you must support the person speaking to you. Support can come in many forms. The trick is to determine which form is appropriate for the given situation. Support does not necessarily mean fixing, advising, or offering a solution. After all, tying a child's shoes for him, when he knows how to do it himself, is not support, it's enabling.

Before offering any kind of support, it's best to ask the person whether or not he or she wants it from you. If the person says yes, then ask, "How can I best support you?" Sometimes the best support is just to listen. Sometimes it's to offer feedback or suggestions. Whatever form of support you offer, it should be one that has the other person's best interests at heart, not yours.

I'm not saying you must go to heroic ends to help anyone who talks to you—that's not a required part of listening—but I am saying that your listening should have a supportive nature. Being a supportive listener means that you encourage others to articulate what they are really thinking and that you are willing and able to point them to a next step, if appropriate and desired—even if that next step might not serve you personally.

The Greatest Gift

We live in lonely, uncommunicative times. It may not seem that way. In fact, a casual observer might conclude that modern humans are totally preoccupied with communicating. (Try prying a smartphone out of the hand of a teenager these days; you're better off petting a snapping turtle.) But, as we now realize, most of our communication has grown shallow, digitized, and tech-driven.

And yet we all hunger for real connections. Studies are now confirming how important human connections are. Not just at home, but in business. Tom Rath, in his book *Vital Friends: The People You Can't Afford to Live Without,* cites scientific research confirming that people are seven times more likely to be engaged (i.e., productive) at their jobs if they have a deep connection with another person at work. He also shows how absence of human connections is linked to problems such as homelessness, failed marriages, and health issues such as obesity. People who don't have real connections feel unloved, abandoned, and hopeless—and act accordingly.

I truly believe this is one of the main reasons we love dogs to the point of cultural obsession: their authenticity, their realness. Dogs force us to relate to them, life-form to life-form, rather than life-form to electronic device to life-form. Around dogs, we feel important. Whenever we're talking to them or spending time with them, they make us the center of their world. They don't try to interrupt us, or outshine us, or distract us, or argue with us. They just beam their incredible attention at us and make us feel that being with us is the best thing in the world.

Some might argue that dogs don't always listen, and that's true; they don't. They listen open and often, and to those whom they respect. That may be why we value dog listening so much. Fortunately for us humans, dogs respect us, even without bacon in hand.

You have the power to make those around you feel the same way a dog makes you feel. You can leave others feeling respected, treasured, and important, simply by listening. And, as a result, you have the ability to improve your relationship with each and every one of those people.

Deep down, you know that focused attention is the greatest gift you can give another person. When you listen to a person, you are saying to him or her, "Right now, you are the most important thing in the world to me. You are more important than making money, doing chores, entertaining myself, and even (yes) talking."

I truly believe you have the power to change your world through listening. That's not an exaggeration or a feel-good fantasy. You have the opportunity every day to make a mark on others and on the world around you. I sometimes wonder why we humans are obsessed with teaching tricks to our dogs. We jump with joy when they learn to stand on two legs or howl the first four notes of "Silent Night." Cute? Beyond cute! But we don't seem to notice the ginormous trick they've been quietly trying to teach us for centuries: how to listen—quietly, compassionately, nonjudgmentally, supportively—like a dog.

I doubt very much whether dogkind as a whole is improved by learning our tricks—how to fetch a newspaper or balance a Milk Bone biscuit on their noses. But I have no doubt whatsoever that humanity would be vastly improved by learning a dog's greatest trick. So the next time someone posts a YouTube video of a dog riding a skateboard (which, according to the law of averages, will probably occur within the next 2.5 seconds), stop and think for a minute about whether you should switch roles for a while. Maybe let dogs teach you for a change.

A human being listening like a dog . . . Now, *that's* a YouTube video that would go viral!

Something to
Chew On . . .

Listening the way I do is the greatest gift
you can give another person.

When I listen, you can feel my support.
I may not understand all of your words, but
you know I have your back.

To listen to a human is to tell him, "Right
now, you are the most important thing in
the world to me.